Small to Tall

How to grow your company

BRODY SWEENEY'S
SMALL TO TALL
how to grow your company from its entrepreneurial roots

Find out how to take your business from Small to Tall and grow your business from its entrepreneurial roots

TAKE TIME OUT TO FORENSICALLY EXAMINE WHERE YOU AND YOUR COMPANY ARE RIGHT NOW - ARTICULATE WHERE YOU WANT TO GET TO - AND REWORK YOUR PLANS TO HELP ACHIEVE YOUR OBJECTIVES

The Course
Based on his new book 'Brody Sweeney's Small to Tall: How to grow your company'. The residential course will be held over 2.5 days (three nights). The course has been designed and will be given by Brody, in a hotel outside Dublin.

The objective of the course is to help those attending gain a better understanding of themselves and their organisations, articulate what success would look like, and plan a strategy that will help get them there.

Who should attend
Founders, owners and chief executives of businesses and organisations who want to grow to the next level of development. This is not a course for people starting a business, but rather for established businesses who want to develop.

For more information log on to www.brodysweeney.ie

Small to Tall

How to grow your company

Brody Sweeney

Gill & Macmillan

Gill & Macmillan Ltd
Hume Avenue, Park West, Dublin 12
with associated companies throughout the world
www.gillmacmillan.ie

© Brody Sweeney 2008
978 07171 4551 5

Index compiled by Cover to Cover
Typography based on design by Make Communication
Print origination by Carrigboy Typesetting Services
Printed by ColourBooks Ltd, Dublin

This book is typeset in Minion 11.5pt on 14pt.

The paper used in this book comes from the wood pulp of
managed forests. For every tree felled, at least one tree is
planted, thereby renewing natural resources.

A CIP catalogue record for this book is available from
the British Library.

5 4 3 2 1

Contents

Connect Ethiopia

Connect Ethiopia is an Irish business initiative, co-founded by myself and Philip Lee. It aims to harness the strength of the business community in one rich country (Ireland) to help the business community in one poor country (Ethiopia).

The rationale for the venture is that countries like Ethiopia are very poor because of the low level of economic activity there. There may be lots of reasons for it, but the reality is still the same: little wealth, jobs or taxes being created.

Traditional charities deal with the effect of this low level of economic activity by, for example, building schools, feeding people, putting AIDS reduction strategies in place, by providing clean water. But there is almost no one dealing with the cause— and that's where Connect Ethiopia comes in.

It seeks to connect Irish business people with their counter-parts in Ethiopia by getting them to travel on one of our 'missions' to Addis Ababa. There they will explore, with their counterparts, opportunities to mentor, to train, to introduce their Ethiopian counterparts to contacts in Ireland, or to invest, and by doing that to get the business community in Ireland to play its part—in a focused way—in poverty eradication.

If you would like to think about joining us in our work, or for further information, log on to *www.connectethiopia.org*

Brody Sweeney
September 2008

Preface

I remember when I realised, to my great joy, that my company was past being a 'start-up'.

Tom Cunningham was the first franchisee of O'Briens back in 1994. Tom was a shrewd accountant from Mayo who truthfully had no interest in becoming a franchisee when I first met him, but was actually after my successful combined newsagents and sandwich bar in Dublin's Stephen's Green Shopping Centre. I should explain that at the time I had two outlets in the Centre: one on the ground floor which contained a newsagents but no seats, and one café on the first floor, with no newsagents.

Running a newsagents had been no part of my business model in O'Briens, but when the managing agents in Stephen's Green Shopping Centre had threatened to throw me out of my then *only* successful store, as the original two-year-and-nine-month lease was up, I had no choice. My only chance of staying on was if I agreed to move to a larger location and open a newsagents as well as a sandwich bar, so I found myself becoming a newsagent in order to keep the business going.

In truth the newsagents did quite well, but I wanted to get back to focusing on developing my chain of sandwich bars. Six years after starting the business, I was ready to franchise it for the first time. The only way I could get money to launch the franchise was by selling my only productive asset—which was this store.

When Tom made me an offer to buy the store, I told him that I was trying to franchise out O'Briens and asked if he would be interested in becoming the first franchisee. I explained to him that I had no long-term plans for a newsagents business, but that I did have for the sandwich bar. I offered him a deal: he could keep the O'Briens name up; I would not charge him any royalty on the newsagents part of the business, and I wouldn't charge him any royalty unless I could sell three franchises.

Tom, with his foresight, took over the business and, when we opened a third franchise, started paying his royalty as agreed.

About a year later Tom came to me and said that he would like to buy the other store that was in Stephen's Green Shopping Centre as well.

That was the moment I realised the business had legs, that it had a future, and that I was on my way. In the immortal words of Sir Alex Ferguson, great teams don't just win championships; they consistently win them.

I had felt that selling the original business to Tom could have been due to good salesmanship on my part, or business naivete on Tom's. But what Tom had demonstrated by coming back to buy a second business was that he was happy with the performance of the first one, comfortable in the business relationship we had, and confident for the future. This was solid and real, and I couldn't have been happier.

Tom went on to run five O'Briens stores and he became one of our largest franchisees before retiring due to ill health. I'll never forget the break he gave me, or the confidence his decisions gave me at a critical stage in the evolution of the business. So to Tom and most of our wonderful franchise partners and good friends over the years, I say thank you from the bottom of my heart, and I dedicate this book to you.

Introduction

By conventional wisdom, entrepreneurs are good at starting organisations but not very good at running them. It's no surprise therefore that of the thousands of new companies that start up each year, very few grow beyond employing a handful of people to become medium or large organisations.

There are lots of reasons why businesses don't grow—from a limited market, to too strong competition, to inadequate financing, to a host of other factors that are plausible on paper at least. But the bottom line is that there is really only one reason why businesses succeed or fail, and that's the attitude and effort of the owner/operator/founder.

WHAT MAKES SOMEONE SUCCESSFUL IN BUSINESS?

Being a successful business person is mostly not about intellectual ability, or about happening on a brilliant idea that the world was just waiting for. In fact I know that if you measured my IQ or that of many other business people, it wouldn't be any higher than that of an average person. It's not brilliance but rather the practical application of common sense that sorts the men from the boys.

For example, it's not rocket science in the food business to know that repeat custom is important, so it just makes common sense to be nice to customers. Nor does it take a genius to figure out that keeping a food store clean sends all the right signals to customers. Leaving these simple examples aside, you could sum up successful people in business under three headings:

- They take personal responsibility for themselves and their business

- They are prepared to do whatever it takes to make the business successful
- They are relentlessly focused on their vision and have a plan to achieve it

In my view, most businesses are a tool to help you reach personal fulfilment.

How you want your business to grow or, indeed, *if* deep down you really want it to grow, are questions you need to address. There's little point in trying to figure out a strategy to take your business on to the next level if you don't know what you want for yourself—if you don't know what your dream is.

Most entrepreneurs do strive to create something great and large, and in the process create the kind of wealth that buys them the freedom to pursue their dreams.

Unfortunately, life has a habit of getting in the way.

WHAT MAKES A BUSINESS SUCCESSFUL?
As we'll explore in *Small to Tall*, great businesses share some simple characteristics:

- A good concept that includes the idea of being really good at one thing
- A good location
- A good owner/operator/founder

The book aims firstly to help you decide whether or not you really do want to grow the business (which may seem like a strange choice) and, secondly, if you do, how you can grow it into something that will help you achieve fulfilment—whatever that looks like for you.

WHO IS THIS BOOK FOR?
Small to Tall is for founders, owners and managers of businesses who want to grow to the next stage of their development. It starts by helping you examine where you are personally, as well

as where your business is. An honest assessment of where you are *now* is the starting point for any changes or improvements you want to make. Having figured that out, the book can then help you to decide where it is you want to be—and by extension where you want your business to be. The final part looks at some ideas for you and your business to help you get there.

Although making a success of your business is ultimately down to yourself, there are also things you can do that will improve your chances of success, and that's what this book is about. It's also designed to be an idea generator. *You* can learn from what *we've* done—expensive mistakes we've made which with hindsight we shouldn't have, and things that have gone well for us that we wished we'd figured out sooner. Bear in mind though that we have some experience of running a sandwich and coffee franchise, and not much else. While many of the ideas in this book are universal, it can't hope to cover all the bases.

For people and businesses who are prepared to do the necessary, *Small to Tall* is designed to smooth your path. After nearly 30 years in business, going from extreme highs to extreme lows, and more importantly by helping and watching hundreds of people to open and run their own businesses under the umbrella of our franchise, I have strong views about how to operate a business and—just as important—how not to.

HOW TO USE THIS BOOK
Small to Tall is designed to work in two ways. Firstly, it's a good read for anyone running a business. It's packed full of ideas for different ways of doing things, some of which I know will be practical and relevant for your business.

Secondly, by taking a notebook and pen, Chapters 2, 3 and 4 are designed to prompt you to reassess where you are going in life, both personally and for your business. To take a few hours out and actually do that in a structured way—which the book helps you to do—is probably as positive an exercise as you could do this year.

You can then use the subsequent chapters to explore the detail of how you will achieve your redefined goals. For example,

Chapter 2 will help you make an honest assessment of where you are with your sales and marketing efforts in the business, which will lead you to Chapter 6, where sales and marketing ideas and strategies are discussed in detail.

Some people have commented to me, from reading my first book, *Making Bread*, that they didn't feel it was completely relevant to them as they weren't in the restaurant or franchise business. While it's true that my personal business experience is limited to these areas, the stories and messages are relevant for all businesses, and I have deliberately written *Small to Tall* with this in mind.

Finally, I wish you continued success on your journey. Remember that it's the quality of the journey that defines your life, not the destination. Thanks for buying the book and by doing so supporting the new passion in my life—Connect Ethiopia.

Chapter 1
You and the Loneliness of the Long-Distance Runner

After almost a year of running O'Briens, and making an idiot of myself in the process, I was finally beginning to get myself sorted out, and the business was getting itself on to a reasonable financial footing. We were still a year behind on our mortgage at home, but this new store should have put things back on an even keel and given me a break from the relentless pressure of trying to keep the show on the road.

I opened our third O'Briens store in Mary Street, Dublin, back in 1999, on a huge high. This was to be the one that would finally put us on a real platform for growth. It needed to be—it couldn't afford to go wrong. I had staked everything on it. In my impetuous fashion I had gone ahead with leasing the store despite having no money to fit it out. But I'd gambled on the cash flow being so strong that I would be able to pay the builder with ease.

After just one week, my enormous high was followed by a huge low. I knew I was in trouble—again. For the stage we were at with the business, it was simply in the wrong location. O'Briens was an upmarket concept, but Mary Street was a downmarket street. I was sick with myself for blowing it spectacularly—yet again. To cap it all, Lulu announced we were to have our first child.

I remember sitting in my van outside the Mary Street store, scared to go in and face people who were looking for money from me. Sinéad O'Connor's hit, 'Nothing Compares 2 U', was playing on the radio. I was at my wits' end, literally cringing from the pressure. There's nothing noble about these times; you're like a cornered rat, so desperate for a way out that you'll consider almost anything to alleviate the pressure.

One Sunday evening not long afterwards, I was flicking through the Sunday papers when I came across an advertisement for Bewley's, then Ireland's most famous coffee house chain. They were looking for a manager for their Dublin cafés. On the spur of the moment, I turned to Lulu and said, 'I'm going to go for that job and if I get it, I'm going to close O'Briens down.' Lulu, wise woman that she was, said nothing.

The next day I applied for the job and was called for an interview. A week later I got a letter in the post: I hadn't got the job.

I went home to Lulu that night. I don't cry often, but I had a tear in my eye as I told her the news. I was at the end of my tether. The business was going down the tubes. As far as I could see it was only a question of time: I would likely be made personally bankrupt, my credit lines would be shot, we stood to lose the house, there was a new baby on the way, and to cap it all I was unemployable.

I had reached my personal low. I thought it was the worst day of my life.

UNDERSTANDING WHAT MAKES YOUR BUSINESS TICK

For most businesses there are three elements which are fundamental to being successful.

The first is concept. A good concept is one where there are enough customers out there willing to pay the prices you charge in order for you to make a consistent profit. In many businesses getting the concept right at the beginning is fraught with difficulty as it is a process of trial and error. But as businesses become more established and the concepts become validated, this becomes less of an issue.

The second issue is one of location. It is essential to be near to your customers. So, for example, in our business in O'Briens, where most of our customer base are young and white collar, the physical location of our stores needs to be in areas where lots of these people congregate to work or play.

In truth, in our business the acquisition of a new premises is a scientific process. So apart from knowing we need to be in a location with lots of young white-collar workers, we also know the kind of rent we can afford to pay, the square footage we require, that we want to be near our competitors, that we're likely to get planning permission for our particular use, that we can afford the work to convert it into an O'Briens, and that it has a certain pedestrian traffic flow past at the critical times for our business.

But location is also important for businesses other than retail. For example, an internet business needs to be 'located' on the web in a way that customers can find it easily; factories need to be near an appropriate supply of labour; lawyers who want to build a family practice locate in the suburbs; and so on.

Location is very difficult to change if it is wrong, and certainly in the early days many of our locations were not good. We paid a very heavy price to change them.

The third element is the person running the business. Actually it is the most important one. Even if you have both the concept and the location right, a poor manager or owner can still screw it up. You could have the best product with the best marketing in the best location, but if your manager/owner is no good, it just doesn't stack up.

So while a lot of this book is about the technical aspects of trying to grow your business from small to tall, in truth the most important element of that is not technical at all—it is really about *you* and your attitude and your beliefs and your values and your smartness.

THE HARDEST THING YOU'LL EVER DO
Statistically, the vast majority of people are incapable of running their own business, which leaves just a small number of us to

generate the economic activity in the country. And that is because for most people it is harder than they are prepared to do.

Nearly everyone is comfortable with the idea of hard work because we nearly all, whether running our own business or not, have to do it at least some of the time. But few who don't run their own show realise the mental stress involved—the fear of failure; the bank manager putting pressure on you to reduce an overdraft when you have no way of doing so. There's the realisation that things, despite external appearances, are not going to plan, and there's the unique knowledge we have that the success or failure of the venture is down to us personally. Ultimately it's no one else's fault.

Even for the small number who do run our own businesses, for most of us it's the hardest thing we'll ever do, particularly at the start of the business. It is also one of the loneliest. You have to make tough decisions, decisions you are probably not used to, and it usually involves spending more money than you were expecting to. As the business grows, this can become hard because sometimes you go off the boil—you just don't have the same passion and enthusiasm for the business as you did when you started it, and you have nobody to help you get that enthusiasm going again except yourself. It is also easy to lose faith in yourself and to believe that you are not really cut out for running your own business. It is particularly hard to admit that you may be wrong about some aspects of the business, and to have the guts to change tack to a different direction—albeit possibly the correct one.

PERSONAL RESPONSIBILITY

If you are already up and running in your business, and you are trying to develop it, you don't need to be told about the importance of taking personal responsibility for all your actions. Personal responsibility is about accepting that what happens in your business is not somebody else's fault: the bank may make you suffer before they lend you money; the market may not be ready for your product at your prices; the competition may murder you; it may be really difficult to employ staff; in particular it might be difficult to employ good salespeople. But at the end of the day the buck stops in only one place—and that is with you.

In our business, it's often more than obvious when, of the three elements in making a successful business, it is the personal element that's wrong.

If you asked someone in our business who *doesn't* take responsibility, what's wrong with their business (and usually there is something wrong), they will tell you:

- The shop is too small or it's too big
- We have too many seats or too few seats
- The competition is too tough
- We're too expensive or we're too cheap
- It's in the wrong location
- I get no support
- It's a crap franchise
- Anyway, nobody's eating thick bread sandwiches any more

The last thing they will say is, 'I'm not managing the business very well' or 'I made a cock-up', and usually that's the real problem. Yes, one of the things mentioned above may contribute to a business's problem, but when you see other businesses operating with the same criteria, and making a success of it, you know that personal responsibility is lacking.

Other people have opinions about your business, about how it operates, what you should sell and what way you should sell it, but you are the only one who has to make the decisions, and if you let popular opinion or other people make decisions for you, not only are you avoiding one of your principal tasks as the developer of the business, but you are heeding popular opinion—and popular opinion is often wrong.

DEALING WITH THE LONELINESS

Some of the loneliest experiences that entrepreneurs go through are the following: thinking that you are the only one going through what you are going through; living with the reality of your own capabilities—which might not be quite as hot as you imagined; trying to deal with a problem that's completely outside your experience; operating in a negative environment where the business is not going as well as anticipated; and losing belief in yourself.

When you are running your own business, it often appears that everyone else is doing okay and you are the only one who is not. I remember in the early days of O'Briens, I was driving my two-seater van around, I still wasn't drawing a salary and was behind in all my personal domestic payments, yet my friends, who had taken regular jobs or had started their own business seemed to be driving around in the latest BMWs, wearing good suits and appeared to have money to burn.

In the middle of the dot-com boom it was particularly lonely. Here we were with our early-stage sandwich and coffee business, struggling to do it right, as best we could, and all around us people seemed to be starting up businesses on the flimsiest of pretexts, putting 'dot com' after their name, somehow persuading investors to back them and becoming millionaires overnight. I remember in the middle of all that frenzy thinking: Is there something wrong with me? Why am I pursuing this 'old-economy' business when all around me people are in new-generation businesses making a fortune? I remember desperately searching for a dot-com angle for our business.

I feel lucky now that I held my nerve and that we kept doing what we were doing. Eventually the dot-com boom collapsed, and many of the millionaires with it, but we kept going with our boring, old-economy business.

Figuring out how to deal with the loneliness isn't easy because we all have different requirements. Many of us just shrug our shoulders and accept it's the price of doing our own thing. For others, becoming involved in a business network, like a chamber of commerce or industry representative body, can provide an appropriate forum to swap war stories with peers and learn from their experience.

For me, getting a mentor took a huge weight off my shoulders. My late mentor, John Gooderham, was a retired senior executive in franchising who had been involved with and ran companies like Dyno-Rod and Prontaprint. John became my foil—I bounced new ideas off him which he was then able to analyse dispassionately and tell me what he would have done. He had the great skill of never telling me what to do; rather, by telling me a story to illustrate a point, he would give me the solution to a problem. He wasn't doing it for the money and so had no pressure to 'perform' or tell me what I might have wanted to hear.

Bringing in a mature head who will give wise advice and who will listen to you, is a great way to relieve loneliness.

KEEPING THE BEST FOOT FORWARD
Reassuring your staff and customers that everything is rosy—when you know things are far from it—is part of a business owner's job. People like being associated with *successful* people and *successful* businesses. Even on days when the pressure of keeping the show on the road is almost more than you can bear, you have to force a smile, maintain a positive attitude and tell everyone how well things are going.

Of course the trick is not to believe your own PR to the extent that you don't fix whatever the problem is.

FAMILY
Remembering that you have a life outside the business, when you are under pressure, is not only difficult for you but also for your nearest and dearest.

Whether you have a family of your own or simply an extended one of brothers, sisters and parents, keeping close to them is not only the right thing to do but also provides a relief and change from the daily grind of your business.

I found that, at my lowest points, spending time with my kids was not only just what I needed but refreshed me for the battles ahead and gave me vital perspective by getting me out of the coleslaw bucket (a term we coined in O'Briens for those of us who are so wrapped up in the day-to-day running of our businesses that we forget why we're there) for a little break. Being there for a partner, who may well be stressed out as a side effect of your business efforts, is vital to keeping a decent relationship going.

HIGHS AND LOWS

As you will know from starting your own venture, nothing really prepares you for the seasonal highs and lows of running your own business. I use the analogy of a marathon runner when speaking about what it is like to start a business and develop it past its infancy.

Somebody who is planning to run a marathon starts preparing maybe six months or a year in advance. You buy your new running gear and running shoes, you start a training programme, you start looking after your diet and you start mentally preparing for the race. You visualise yourself as a winner. As the race approaches, that level of preparation intensifies, until eventually the day comes when you find yourself on the starting line ready to start the race.

Just before the race you're feeling strong with a very positive attitude about how well you are going to do in the race and that you're going to beat your personal best. You may have family or friends around you wishing you well, telling you that you are going to do the business. You know the amount of preparation and time you have put into getting ready for it, and you start the race on a huge high.

The gun goes and you set off with your head held high and your chest out. Five miles out and you're going well. That's fine for the first 10 or 15 miles, but for most amateur runners, at around 16 or 17 miles they start to get into a bit of trouble. The blood sugar level in your body falls, you start to get weak, your legs turn to jelly and a lot of amateur runners now start to lose self-belief.

They think to themselves, maybe I am not going to be able to finish; maybe I haven't done enough training; maybe I'm not good enough to run a marathon; maybe I'm too old. Experienced marathon runners talk about this stage in the race; they call it the 'Wall' (which you hit) because it's almost like running into a wall.

Now for a small number of amateur marathon runners this is the point where they actually do give up. They just say, 'I have had enough . . . I've done my best', and they stop. But for the vast majority of runners it is only a stage in the journey and somehow they get past 17/18/19 miles. By the time they reach 20 or 21 miles they are starting to get a bit of strength back into their legs, the blood sugar levels are starting to come back up a bit, they start realising that the end is not far away, and they get back their self-belief.

Compare that with starting a business. In a franchise business like O'Briens, if you're a new franchisee, we help you prepare for the new business start-up well in advance of when it is to open. You do practical and theoretical training about how you might run it; we do a business plan with you so you can have a roadmap for where the business is going to go; we help you acquire premises and fit it out to the latest style. We assist in recruiting your staff; we set up deals with suppliers; we organise a marketing launch and a push; and eventually we get to the opening day.

Our franchisees usually get to the opening days, despite being tired, on a huge high—because only they know the amount of preparation and work that has gone into getting them ready, and they have a personal belief in themselves that they are going to have the most successful O'Briens business ever.

They are usually surrounded by their families and friends saying, 'You're fantastic . . . Congratulations. You are going to be a great success.' And that franchisee is sitting looking at his brand-new, shiny shop thinking, 'I'm here; it's mine; I can touch it—I can feel it—I can see it.'

And so they start their new business on a huge high. But as inevitably as night follows day, huge highs are followed by huge lows. It is hard to predict when it happens in business, but often it is three or four months into the new business. Our new owner is physically exhausted from standing on a hard, stone floor for 16–17 hours a day, six or seven days a week. They may have lost weight; maybe they are not seeing very much of their family. It is quite conceivable that their sales are not where they thought they would be, or they are having difficulty controlling their margins, and that has an impact on their cash flow. Maybe they are under pressure from the bank. They could have lost weight and they are never at home and perhaps not contributing to the family in the way they did before; they may have somebody at home feeling a little resentful, saying, 'I told you it would never work' or 'I told you not to give up the job.' And at that stage many of our franchisees hit a real low. They hit their wall in the marathon sense and they start to think: maybe I am not cut out to be a self-employed business person; maybe I am not good enough; maybe the location isn't good enough; maybe our prices are too high—they start to look for excuses.

But like our marathon runners, hitting an extreme low is only part of the journey to getting it right. Because, as inevitable as is hitting an extreme low, it is followed, of course, by another high—maybe not as high as the opening day, but a high nevertheless.

So, after hitting the new high, they then fall back down into a new low, but not quite as low as the first one, and the highs and lows become more evened out and the business smoothes out into a kind of equilibrium.

The point of this story, of course, is that if and when you hit an extreme low and things seem to be going against you, remember that this is just part of the journey to getting it right—it is not a destination in its own right.

THE VALUE OF HAVING A MENTOR

If there is one thing I could have changed in the early years of my business it would be to have taken in a mentor from outside to avoid some of the sillier decisions I made. Mentors tend to be experienced people, perhaps in your sector, who are retired and therefore don't have a particular axe to grind but who nevertheless want to keep their hand in the business.

The real value of having a mentor is that when you are reaching important decisions in the life of your business, you have somebody to bounce them off and so decisions aren't made on an impetuous or rushed basis but rather are carefully considered as to the short-term and the long-term impacts they are likely to have. John Gooderham, my mentor referred to previously, provided me with just the sounding board I needed as well as a dispassionate voice in my sea of enthusiasm.

Contrary to popular belief, mentors are widely available. Many older businesspeople who have much to offer are only waiting to be asked to help and, in my experience, truly love the involvement without the pressure.

THE VALUE OF PEER SUPPORT

Because running a business is such a lonely occupation for many of us, joining a network of people in a similar situation can be a great idea—you can discuss your war stories or the problems you are facing, and perhaps somebody in the group has already experienced that problem and dealt with it in their own way. The benefit, therefore, is twofold—firstly it is practical because somebody may have a practical solution to a problem you are experiencing, and secondly it takes away the loneliness because you are now sharing your problem with somebody who is neither directly competing with you, nor are they a customer or an employee.

Looking back with time and perspective on those days around opening our Mary Street store, I realise that that day wasn't the worst one in my life. In fact it was one of the luckiest. Had I been given the job with Bewley's, I would almost certainly have closed down O'Briens, and it wouldn't have gone on, with the people it did, to enjoy the success that it has. I would probably be a salaried manager in a catering company now, and I wouldn't have been given the opportunity to write this book—and most likely, you wouldn't have been interested in reading it!

Brody's 3 ideas for dealing with the loneliness

- Take personal responsibility for your actions
- Join a group of your business peers
- Get a mentor

Chapter 2

Where are You? Where is your Business Right Now?

About seven years ago, not long after my fortieth birthday—which was a bit of a wake-up call—I awoke in the middle of the night in a sweat. The business had started to go well: we had received our first outside investment, I was drawing a regular salary and life looked good. But here I was working my ass off to make the business a success, when all the things outside the business which were important to me were withering away because I wasn't giving them enough attention. I decided there and then that I was going to do something about it. Not for me the epitaph, 'He made a lovely sandwich' or 'He was always first in to the office'. I wanted something more than success in business, even though that is hugely important to me. I wanted success in life or, as I worked out for myself, to live a life where I achieved my potential, whatever that looked like for myself—and it is different for everybody. Up to that point I had never really thought about why I was doing what I was doing. I was like Pavlov's dog—I was just doing it like an automaton.

When I did think about it, being successful in business was like a tool I could use to reach my goals. Business provided the satisfaction of achievement, the community of like-minded spirits striving to achieve a goal, and of course the money to fund a comfortable lifestyle. Running your own business gives you a freedom you could never have as an employee, and you can use that freedom to go off and try different things—in my case running for a seat in the Dáil, writing a book, and starting up a charity.

I started reorganising my life by asking myself three simple questions:

- Where am I now—and where is my business at now?
- Where do I want to be—and by extension where do I want my business to be?
- How am I going to get there—and how am I going to get the business there?

The objective of this chapter is to take that first point and make an honest assessment of who *you* are, and where you and your business are right now.

Before we can start to think about what we're going to do to sort ourselves out, we need to have a platform or benchmark against which to measure ourselves.

None of us has a perfect life; none of us runs a perfect organisation. In this chapter we're going to try and make a completely honest assessment of ourselves and our organisation. It stands to reason therefore that aspects of this exercise are going to make us uncomfortable, as there are parts of each one of us, or things we're doing in our business, that we're not comfortable with or that we don't like.

I suggest that this is a good time to get out a pen and paper and start to take some notes on the subject matter we're discussing here. It's also possible that ideas will come to you that you might want to use later.

You may wonder why, in a business development book like this, I would want to spend so much time on your personal development, which on the surface doesn't seem related. In fact your personal development and the development of your business are inextricably linked. You can't have a healthy and thriving business without taking care of the health and well-being of the business driver.

We'll start by looking at some of the things that influence the way we behave as a person.

WHERE ARE YOU AT RIGHT NOW?

Part 1

Where am I on the Wheel of Life?

There is an old, clichéd way of looking at how you spend your time which you may have come across before. Nevertheless it's an easy way of looking graphically at areas of your life which you know need more attention.

In Tibet, the Wheel of Life is a representation of Buddhist teaching about getting your life in harmony. It helps identify areas to which you need to pay attention in order to achieve that balance. It goes without saying that if the wheel is unbalanced, it won't go very far.

Fill out your wheel by taking each segment and marking on it a line which is parallel to the rim of the wheel. The centre of the wheel is zero and means you are giving that area of your life absolutely no attention. Ten is the rim of the wheel and means you are giving that area everything. Mark your line to show where you are in that area of your life on the wheel.

The eight segments which make up the wheel for most poeple are:

- Relations with a partner
- Friends and family
- Personal finance
- Business
- Personal development
- Fun
- Health
- Contribution

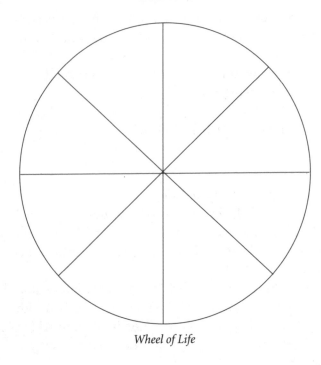

Wheel of Life

Of course bumpy wheels don't roll very smoothly, and this is an interesting metaphor for our lives.

Personal finances

My father used to say, 'It doesn't matter how much money I earn, my lifestyle always costs a steady 10 per cent more than my income.' Where are you with your personal finances at the moment? Is your take-home pay adequate to support the sort of life you lead or would like to lead? Are you comfortable with your mortgage? What state of indebtedness are you in? Leaving your mortgage aside, are you comfortable with your overdraft (is it being used for seasonal ups and downs, or is there a hard-core of long-term debt in there)? What about your credit card, car loans, HP payments?

Are you able to manage your domestic bills, school fees, holidays etc? Are you saving enough? What's the realistic value of your shares in the business? Is it where you think it should be?

Make a note of where you are right now and, more importantly, which areas of your personal finances you would like to improve.

Relationships

How would you characterise your principal relationships at the moment? That includes not only close ones—with a partner, family or friends—but also the main ones you have in your work. Are you giving these relationships enough time? Which ones need more attention than others?

Health and fitness

How is your health and fitness at the moment? Think about your ideal self for a moment. Are you as healthy as you want to be? Have you habits that are affecting your health? How much exercise are you getting? Are there things about your health and fitness you have been putting off?

What are the things about yourself that you would like to change?

When did you last have a major check-up? Do you drink excessively or smoke?

Make a note of those areas you would like to do something about.

Personal development

What is your time off like at the moment? Is your work-life balance good? What about sports and recreation—are you taking some time for them? What about 'me' time—are you giving yourself any? How about further study or training—do you need some, or would you like to do some?

Fun

What are you doing to enjoy life at the moment? How much time off work do you take? What about working weekends or nights? What about holidays? What about doing things together as a family or with your closest friends?

Contribution

I read a quote in a book of quotations which I absolutely loved: 'The ultimate test of a leader is, because you lived, life is better.' How do you give back at the moment? Do you contribute cash, volunteer, coach in sports, look after an elderly relative etc? Are you involved in your local business organisations? Do you mentor anyone?

Part 2

WHERE IS MY BUSINESS RIGHT NOW?

Let's have a look at our business now and where it is, as opposed to where we would like it to be. As with our personal analysis, this should be a completely honest, warts-and-all appraisal of your business. In particular we want to look at aspects of the business you're less than happy about, things that need fixing. Make a note of these aspects as you go along, to prompt yourself later, but also make a note of new ideas as they occur to you.

The list below is not comprehensive. There may be other areas of your business that are unique to you, so don't hold back if something occurs to you.

My organisation

Describe what it is your company does in 50 words. It's interesting that when we need to articulate what we do in just a few words, many of us struggle to find the words that encapsulate our idea.

Management

How am I managing? Am I covering all the areas I should be? What areas should I be spending more time on? Am I delegating enough? What areas should I be spending less time on? Are the different areas of the business organised correctly? Should I reorganise it? Am I keeping stakeholders/lenders informed of what's going on? Are we holding regular meetings? Is there an agenda? Do we stick to time?

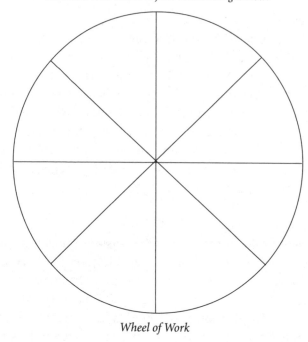

Wheel of Work

Wheel of Work

As with our Wheel of Life analysis earlier, it's really worth doing the same exercise in a work context.

Some suggested headings and prompt notes are written below, but you can substitute different headings if they are more appropriate for your business. The point is to identify which areas you are giving the most attention, or the least. The list of ideas is not comprehensive, but designed to get you thinking.

- Innovation
- Finance
- Sales and marketing
- Operations
- People
- Purchasing
- Planning
- Communication

Finances

How am I capitalised? Do I need more? How much do I need? Do I need to swap debt for equity? How are relations with my financial backers? How am I managing the money? Is cash control okay? What about leakage—being ripped off? Are we charging enough to get a return? How's cash flow? What could I do to make it better? What about debtor and creditor management? Have we got a budget? Is it realistic? Am I happy with our financial advisers/auditors? Are our pricing/estimating formulas up to date/appropriate?

Sales and marketing

How are our sales at the moment versus our budgets or plans? Are they too seasonal—should I be taking steps to make them less so? Have we a plan to increase sales in the business? What are we actually doing about increasing sales? What methods are we using to sell? How effective are they? Is there accountability in our sales team; have we worked out our sales formula yet (see Chapter 6)? Are we doing any PR; is there a plan; are we getting appropriate coverage? What about advertising—what are we doing in this area? Is it appropriate and cost effective? Could we be doing it better or differently? Are we doing it in-house or out? Should we be doing it in-house or out? What is our online strategy on the internet?

Purchasing

Is the way we organise our purchasing efficient? Are there suppliers out there we need to change? How are relations with our other suppliers? Are we seeing new suppliers on a regular basis so that we can compare them with our existing suppliers? Are we sharing our plans with suppliers? Have we trained them as to how we want to do business?

Planning

Are we spending sufficient time planning? Have we a five-year plan? Have we a plan for this year? Are we monitoring how we are doing against our objectives?

People

What's our staff turnover like at the moment? How are my relationships with the key people in my business? Am I spending enough time with my key people? Am I visible/accessible to my non-key people? Are they adequately trained? Are my key repetitive processes manualised?

Is there someone who's just not working out whom I haven't been dealing with? Why are they not working out? Have I got a good bonus/incentive scheme in place? Is there a personal development plan in place for key people? Do they know how much I value them?

Are management accountable? Are we giving younger people a chance to shine?

Innovation

What are we selling? Is it an appropriate mix? Are there lines we're making no money on, or that are inappropriate for where the business is now? What's the standard of our products compared to our ideal? Are they really excellent and best suited for purpose? How are they packaged and sold? Do we need to upgrade in this area? Are we coming up with new ideas at the moment? Are we monitoring the competition?

Communications

How are we communicating with the key stakeholders in our business?

- Shareholders
- Management
- Staff
- Suppliers
- Customers
- Non-customers
- The public

Corporate social responsibility

How do I treat my people? Am I proud of my interaction and behaviour with the people with whom I work? Are we knowingly damaging the environment with our practices? Are we segregating waste appropriately in the business? Are we dealing with complaints properly? Are our expectations about what our staff can do realistic? Do we treat customers fairly? Do we treat suppliers fairly? Do we support a good cause as a business? Do we support our community?

You should be making notes as ideas occur to you. Similarly, make a note of areas for improvement or areas that need attention, remembering that there may be more issues related to your specific business that are not covered here.

If you have done this exercise clinically and diligently, you are already on the way to making the changes you need. Realising where you are is a starting point.

Brody's 3 ideas for finding out where you are

- Make an honest assessment of where you are personally and where your business is
- Note areas of your business and your life that need attention, or fixing, and write them down
- Commit to getting your wheels to run less bumpily

Chapter 3

Your Vision for the Future

DREAMS

Like all people growing up, I had a vivid imagination about what my future would be like and, more particularly, how I could emulate one of my heroes. Childhood visions went from playing in the orchestra at the Gaiety Theatre to captaining Ireland as we won the Grand Slam, to rescuing my parents from their sinking ship. My first vision of adulthood was to imagine myself as rich and famous!

I well remember my dream as a senior school student. It was to be very popular, with loads of money, an ability to get all the girls and drive a fantastic car; in my immature ways, it seemed terribly simple. Of course my vision has matured since then, but my vision was what got me started in my first business venture, and that initial vision has led me to where I am today.

Like me, you will have started with your own vision. It may not have been well defined then, but you dreamt of something that has ultimately led you to where you are. We are where we are now: somewhere on the way to achieving our vision, or indeed responding to some *new* vision that we have had since then.

As we look to grow from small to tall, it is a great time to reflect on where we are right now, where we want to be, and how we are going to get there. This section is all about where we want to be; most importantly, where we want to be personally—for ourselves. And then how we are going to use the business to deliver on that aspiration.

I have always been conscious that I am only here once, and life isn't a dress rehearsal. This is it. This is for real. It's the only chance we're going to get. My personal dream has evolved from my desire to be rich and famous, to something more appropriate for me now. And as I draw my last breath my dream is to say, 'That was a great life' according to my values.

Do you ever think about why most businesses stay small? And they do. For the vast majority of those who start businesses, their businesses don't grow very much. Sometimes this is simply because they are incapable of growing big. But often I think it's because of a complete lack of clarity about where they are trying to go, in other words, a lack of vision.

During my recent foray into politics, I was asked to take part in a survey of election candidates who were standing for the first time. Part of the questionnaire revolved around why I was going into politics. In particular, I was asked to list specifically five reasons why I wanted to become a politician. Having thought about it a great deal before the question was asked, I did not have a great problem coming up with an answer. I had thought fairly clearly about why I wanted to do what I was doing, and had very specific reasons for making the attempt.

After I had completed the questionnaire, the researcher, who was doing the survey as part of a masters in political science, said I was one of the very few aspiring politicians he had interviewed who actually had a compelling reason to get into politics. He said the majority of people were very woolly about why they were going into it. There were a lot of indistinct answers—they wanted to serve the public; they wanted to represent their community; it seemed like a good career. Very few, however, could give a specific reason or reasons as to why they wanted to enter politics.

This group of aspiring politicians could very easily be aspiring businesspeople. A lot of them, for a variety of reasons, end up running their own business without compelling reasons as to why they are doing so. My perception is that if you are not absolutely clear about why you are doing it, or whether there is a good reason for doing it, then it is very hard to achieve a meaningful outcome.

What we are going to attempt to do here is to define *why* you are doing *what* you are doing, and really get into *where* you want to go personally, and then by extension with your business. I have deliberately put the 'personally' bit first, because apart from the sense of satisfaction that developing a business gives you, for many of us a business is essentially a tool by which you can achieve a personal vision. If you can begin to define why you are doing what you are doing, where you want to go personally, and then plan how you are going to do it, it should make the whole process of planning more realistic, more achievable and simpler.

So before we attempt to re-do our plans, we are going to try and re-do our vision—in other words, we are going to try and visualise the future. Get that pen and notebook ready!

VISUALISATION
Visualisation is a technique used by modern athletes. They realise that if they want to compete effectively, not only must they be technically fit and competent for their particular sport, but their mental attitude must be right—it is just as important as fitness or technical ability.

A modern golfer like Irishman Pádraig Harrington, in the top ten in world terms, uses visualisation as part of his preparation for big competitions. He literally goes around the golf course mentally before every big game, playing it. In his imagination he plays every hole and every shot, and sees himself in a winning position. It is one of the techniques he uses to remain in the top ten in his game.

Visions change from time to time. As you can see from my initial vision of my future in terms of fame and wealth early on in my life, this has now changed for me to a more mature sense of what I want for myself. I know for example that my vision changed substantially when I became part of a family and started having children. I would say I have refined my vision now to a single line. My personal vision is that I fulfil my potential, whatever that potential is. And that defines how I try to lead my life.

What I propose to do here is encourage you to define your own personal mission statement. Generally speaking I hate mission statements. You used to see them all the time in the reception area of businesses, where they proclaimed some lofty ideals for the business to which nobody paid a blind bit of notice. If you are going to write a mission statement, it has to be real; it has to be achievable; and it has to be something to which you can personally subscribe. The personal mission statement should encapsulate your values and your ideals and, having captured them, it should help you articulate your vision for the future.

To have a clear vision of your future brings all sorts of benefits. For example, you can have measurable goals and milestones—satisfying to achieve, as well as giving you something to stretch to and try and reach. You can also have absolute clarity of purpose. You know where you are trying to go and why you are trying to get there. Having a clear vision helps you focus, and focus brings its own rewards—for example, not getting distracted. If someone comes up with a proposal, you are able to see whether or not it fits into your vision of the world.

Let me give you a business example of this. In our business, O'Briens, our vision is to be the best in the world at selling sandwiches and coffee. It's a very simple vision which we struggle to achieve. If you shop with us on a regular basis, you will realise that we are not there yet. In fact in many ways we're a very long way from achieving our goal. Yet the mission statement gives us absolute clarity about what we're trying to do.

For instance, I used to get asked frequently to go into different businesses with different people. I recognised that my strengths and knowledge are in the field of franchising and so, if the business idea didn't have a franchising component, I wasn't interested. By being clear about this, I didn't distract myself by thinking, for example, 'Why didn't I buy property when prices were low?' Property wasn't my business. Having the clear vision of where we want to be, or what we want to be, means that you can, when proposals like these come up, be really clear about rejecting them, as ultimately they just do not help you achieve your goal.

Once you have articulated your vision for your business, it is then up to you to lead your troops in the direction you have visualised. This brings its own issues; for example, it is like your baby. In a healthy business, the stakeholders will all have different views about how the business should develop and operate. If it is your baby, and you believe your vision is correct, then it is up to you to make sure that your view prevails. By and large businesses do not get from small to tall by being a democracy. They get there because you have the guts and leadership qualities to see your vision through to the end. As a visionary you also set the tone for the organisation—it is after all *your* beliefs and *your* values that people are being asked to sign up to. You also become the brand guardian. You are like the policeman for your company, the officer who makes sure that the rules that you have set are followed, that the vision you have articulated gets followed, and your troops do not go off on a meaningless tangent. You provide the leadership—the leadership that ensures your troops understand what you are all trying to achieve and that they are willing participants in the venture.

PERSONAL VALUES AND BELIEFS

Before you cast your visions, both personal and business, in stone, let's look at what is important to you—including your personal values and beliefs—in other words, what it would take for you to make a great life. To help you do this, imagine you are sitting down in a pub on a January evening with your best friend. You are talking about what a wonderful year you had last year. It was the best year of your life, because it all came together; your dreams and aspirations were realised and you felt fulfilled.

What did you say to your friend? How did you describe this exceptional year in your life?

Be bold; imagine you are a child again. You had no problem with your imagination then. And before we start, what is a vision? My vision is when I look into the future and picture how I would like it to be. So for this exercise, let's really dream about what your life would be like, say, five years from now. That's the year you're describing to your best friend. What we are going to do is dream about the different aspects of your life which are important to you. It's not a definitive list; there may be other areas or other things that are more important to you than what we are looking at here, but you will get the general gist.

Family
Let's start by dreaming about your family. So if we were dreaming five years from now, what would that look like? Would you have a partner? Would you be married? How many children would you have? Would you want to have any? What would you do with your time? Presumably you would dream of being happy. Where would you live? What about your extended family—what sort of relationship would you have with them? How often would you see them? What about your close friends—how often would you see them? What would you do together? How would you celebrate your birthday in five years' time?

Finances
Let's visualise your finances now in five years' time—your cash flow. Would you have your mortgage paid off? You would need enough to put the kids through college, probably, and perhaps pay a deposit on a house for them. What about your long-term financial goals? You might want to sell the business for a big lump sum. What would that sum look like? How much would it be? Would you want to fund a great pension, and maybe *not* look at selling the business in five years? Would you like to have the money to travel more, or to have a hobby like owning a big yacht or helicopter, or collecting vintage cars?

Personal development

Imagine where your personal development might bring you in five years' time. If you were to wave a magic wand and see into the future, would you like to do further education, or more training in some specific aspect of your business? Would you like to have a life coach? What about going back to college? What about sport—do you like sports? Do you like being part of a team? What would you like to be doing in five years sportswise? What about your spiritual well-being—is religion important to you, or meditation, or your attitude to others? What about time off—how much time would you like to have for yourself and your partner and your family, or for your hobbies, or for your personal development?

Health

What state of health would you like to be in five years from now? How fit would you like to be? What will you be eating and drinking? Will you eat more or less? Will you drink more or less? Will you have given up something that is bugging you right now? Looking five years hence, will your lifestyle be crushing you into bad health or will you take time out to look after your body and your physical health?

Contribution

What will you be doing to give something back in five years' time? Will you be involved in some charity like the Lions Club or will you be making a financial contribution to a charity you hold dear? What about *pro bono* work? Will you be doing some of that for a worthwhile cause? What about mentoring, or perhaps coaching a kids' football team? Would you like to be doing any of that in five years' time?

BUSINESS

To help you deliver on all that, where will your business be in five years? What will that look like? Firstly, start by trying to define, in numbers, what your business might look like over the long term. Remember, we are dreaming of a happy life here, so don't hold back. At the same time we do need to be realistic. So here we are looking forward five years from now. Try to define your business in terms of its size, its profitability, how much money it will be making, and finally what it will it be worth—its value.

What business are we in?
What do we do, and how do we do it? What are we going to need to change about what we're doing right now to achieve our vision?

I want our business to be the best in the world at . . .
We will do many things, but if we're asked about what we're absolutely best at, most passionate about, what one thing we do defines us as a business?

Who will the key people be?
Who will be running the business? How will the staff be organised? Who will my mentor be?

Sales and marketing
Who will our top customers be? How will the sales mix be broken up? How much business will come each year from existing customers, and how much from new? What methods will you be using to sell?

Planning
How will your planning process work?

• Specific planning
• Staff development
• Long-term planning

And while we are on definitions, let's define *why* you are looking ahead. Is it because you do not want to be a boss any more?

Could it be you're trying to build a legacy to hand on, or indeed maintain an existing legacy that you have inherited? Could it be that you are after high income, that you want to earn a lot of money in five years, or do you want to have a valuable asset that you could sell? Or is it about lifestyle—you may want to work at your own pace or you may want to work with your own partner? *Why* are you doing *what* you are doing?

To finish with definitions, what is the endgame? What is the ultimate objective of this business? Could it be that you'll sell it all in five years and retire? Could it be that you'll have it in such a position that you can take a back seat, and travel and fulfil other dreams? Could it be like my own objective, which was to have a healthy business in five years' time so that I would have the freedom to decide how I wanted to live the rest of my life? If I wanted to continue with the business, I could decide to do so. If I wanted to do something else, I would have the choice to do that also. Then, finally, as we round out on our definitions section, how can we define what it is that we could be the *best* at in business.

These questions, these ideas for visualising yourself and your business, are designed to stimulate your thought processes. When you have answered these questions and thought through your vision, then we will be ready to plan.

You can start this exercise right now by getting a blank sheet of paper and perhaps starting with headings like the samples I have listed below.

Under each heading you could start by thinking, 'In five years' time, under the heading of Family, I would like . . . ' and so on.

There are no right or wrong answers for you, any more than these are the right or wrong headings for you. You are unique, and your view of the world and your dreams and aspirations are yours alone.

Personal headings	Business headings
• Family	• Finance
• Relationships	• Sales and marketing
• Health and lifestyle	• Operations
• Personal development	• People
• Contribution	• Purchasing
• Finances	• Planning
• The business	• Communications

Brody's 3 ideas on visualisation

- Try and define what you think would make you personally fulfilled
- Imagine and articulate how your successful business will look in five years' time
- Imagine your business is a tool to help you achieve your personal dreams

Chapter 4
Planning Long Term and Short Term

THE IDEA BEHIND PLANNING

The original vision for my business was to open 1,000 stores and be the most successful franchise in Europe. Almost 20 years after starting the business with that vision, we have around 300 stores but a lot less than 1,000. In that sense you could say we have failed. But I'm absolutely convinced that if we didn't have a big dream—and the plans to go with it—we would probably never have opened more than two or three stores.

Having thought through in the vision chapter what you want for yourself, and then by extension for your business, and then having sorted your goals under different headings, you can now start to plan *how* you are going to achieve them. A long-term vision for a business can seem daunting. To visualise a business with 1,000 stores when you only have three is a stretch too far. The old management story of eating an elephant comes to mind. At first glance it seems impossible to eat an elephant and indeed it probably is, but if you break the elephant down into platefuls which you then serve to people who eat the platefuls one forkful at a time, it's actually quite possible to eat the elephant.

EATING AN ELEPHANT

Think of the long-term vision for your business as an elephant. Break it down firstly into big pieces, for example, the thigh and head, which might equate to a year! Then divide *these* big chunks into platefuls—the months of the year, and finally into forkfuls—the individual objectives within a period. You get the idea. To watch ourselves progressing motivates us. It is a fantastic motivator to see yourself eating one forkful at a time, and mentally ticking it off your to-do list. It will spur you on to try even harder to eat the whole bloody thing!

In terms of your long-term planning, there are really three types of plan which equate with the elephant and the plateful and the forkful. The first one is your long-term plan—your blue sky vision of where the business could actually be. This is the elephant. The platefuls are the big picture ideas within the blue sky. For example, a blue sky idea might be 1,000 stores. The plateful would be the 50 stores we have to do this year, to make that happen. The forkfuls are your specific objectives—these are hugely detailed, where other people take responsibility for various objectives with full buy-in from your staff. They are also immediate and achievable.

In this book we don't go into the detail of preparing business plans because there are literally dozens of books out there which do just that in the greatest of technical detail. What I want to do instead is to give you some general ideas about the practical aspects of your specific business planning, over and above the technical aspects. You see, the idea behind planning is not just to put in place a document that your bank is going to believe and on the strength of which give you money, but rather for you to articulate *your* vision for the business—to put it down in writing.

This can then be used as a tool to share with your stake-holders, for example, with your staff to get their buy-in, or with the banks because you need to get money from them, or with shareholders who might potentially invest in the business.

It could be used to show a potential landlord how the business would operate, to convince him that you have thought through all the issues. Indeed, it can also persuade a supplier to supply you.

FIGURING OUT YOUR GOALS AND ASPIRATIONS

Your plan contains your goals and aspirations, and that's important in the sense of giving yourself a yardstick by which to measure performance—not only yours, but also the performance of the people who work with you.

I have already suggested that to operate without goals is pointless. Essentially, your business plan gives you a roadmap to show the directions in which you should travel to reach the ultimate destination—your vision. Your roadmap will be an imperfect one which will change as you react to events of the day, and in that sense, some people may feel it's a somewhat pointless exercise doing it if it's going to change so dramatically. But anyone who tries to travel without a map will tell you that any map is good; even if it is not terribly accurate, it is certainly a lot better than no map at all.

Having said that, we need to try and make our plans as accurate as we possibly can. We also recognise, of course, that something we write down now that we think is going to happen in five years' time is, at best, an educated guess but, more realistically, is a fantasy.

It is possible, however, to be fairly accurate with what can happen in the year ahead.

DON'T TRY TO MAKE THE PLAN FIT

One danger of preparing plans is that there is a very human temptation to try and make the plan fit with our reality. For example, when I was opening our first O'Briens, the money available to me was about IR£50,000. In reality, I knew the shop was going to cost about IR£75,000 to open, but I didn't have it. Nor did I have any hope of getting it. I therefore rewrote the plan to show the start-up costs for that shop as £50,000—even though it wasn't true. That meant I was behind from the start.

Making sales projections fit expectations, or making capital budgets fit the available cash, is really not doing yourself or your fledgling business any service. Wish lists (what you would like to happen) as opposed to real lists (what is likely to happen) are two separate and completely different things. Business plans should be built on real lists, not wish lists. I offer that piece of wisdom with one small proviso: you do need to be realistic, but you also need to be optimistic. There needs to be an upside. Your bank, which will be one of the stakeholders with a very keen interest in your business plan, may decide not to back you if you are too realistic.

WRITTEN PLANS AND FINANCIAL PLANS

Articulating our plans so others can share them means we need to write down a written description of what we want to do, together with timelines, and a plan for what will happen with the money in the business so that we can identify potential problems or indeed opportunities. The written plan is the story of what we think will happen (at best an educated guess), broken down by areas of responsibility and control. The financial plan is the story of what we think will happen with the numbers, showing where you will need money or investment in the business or, potentially, where you are going to throw up cash surpluses. The financial plan should also give you an idea of what the most lucrative parts of the business may be. Most importantly, when you do the draft plan, it should show how you may need to adjust your costs to fit in with the available revenues.

START WITH THE BLUE SKY

The blue sky, as we saw in the vision chapter, is your dream about what could happen to make this a business that you could be proud of, and a business that could satisfy your financial aspirations. It is very difficult to be prescriptive because we all have such wildly different ideas, but mine was to open 1,000 stores and to have the best franchise system in Europe with the most profitable franchisees. When I articulated that vision, it meant for me initially that if I achieved those goals, I would consider myself to have been a success, and it certainly would have satisfied my financial aspirations.

For you, why not think in terms of, 'If everything went perfectly I would be the owner of a company worth €x with y number of staff and be the best in the world at z.'

PLANNING FOR THE LONG TERM

Having written down and articulated our blue sky vision of where we are going to go in the future, it is now time to put that into real terms, that is to say, to plan what we think could happen over the next five years to help us achieve our blue sky goal.

One thing that governments and, indeed, large public companies get blamed for is an absence of long-term planning. In a government's case they have to face an electorate, probably every five years, who may not be pleased that their taxes have been raised to pay for some long-term public service project, even if in the long term it is for the public good. Public companies face shareholders and analysts who tend to think in terms of months and quarters, not in terms of years.

This is an important point because, if you constantly go for the easy short-term win, it is hard to build lasting value. That is why, even though you recognise that detailed planning has one year or at most two years' validity, after which it is not based on reality, the act of thinking about planning—and how you would operate your business to achieve your long-term goals— definitely *is* based on reality.

Start by writing down a five-year objective for the business; that brings us substantially along the way to reaching our business vision. For example, 'In five years I would like to be in a business that is making €1 million per annum, that is worth €10 million and is a desirable business for anybody to buy and the best in the country at selling sandwiches and coffee. After the first five years I would like to have opened 100 outlets.' It could be anything in your business: the point is it is a meaty objective that you will really have to work hard and push yourself to achieve. You need to be specific about the type of business yours will be, and particularly what it is in the world you are going to be best at. 'I want to be rich and successful' is not a specific vision. Your financial aspirations also need to be specific, with the same proviso: that any projections more than one year in advance are really for the fairies. The point is that you are *going* for something. And it's something you can share with other people, and it is measurable.

PLANNING FOR THE SHORT TERM
Planning for the short term is planning for the next year—what is going to happen in the coming 12 months. Obviously a short-term plan contains a huge amount of detail, which is divided into areas of responsibility and an appropriate timeline. Lots of good books will show you the details of business planning, so I don't intend to go into them here.

The short-term plan is what is going to be of most interest to your shareholders, and perhaps your bankers. This is because, although they'll be interested in the long term and will want to share your vision for the future of the business, they will know from experience that if you can't manage the short-term situation, there won't be a long term.

Because they will be much more interested in the immediate plan than in the long-term one, your plan needs to be clearly understood, believable and with clearly defined financial and operational goals that your people can sign up to, particularly in terms of taking responsibility to achieve their own part of the overall goal.

COMMUNICATING AND GETTING BUY-IN FROM YOUR STAKEHOLDERS
In our early years especially, I used every opportunity I could to shout the O'Briens vision from the rooftops. My thinking was that the more the people around me knew what we were trying to achieve, the more likely it was that they would understand the

level at which they would be expected to perform, and so be more motivated to achieve.

I have ended up with egg on my face a few times: 'We will have opened 1,000 stores over the next five years' is one that caused me a little embarrassment, but the risk of being wrong about your predictions is heavily outweighed by people knowing what it is they are part of.'

Buy-in from your team

There's also the fact that you can't do it on your own, so sharing the plan and getting buy-in from your team, particularly your staff, is crucial in terms of the role they have to play—their responsibilities and your expectations of them. Setting clear plans in the short term will help you allocate responsibility to the various people working with you.

Of course, you need to be realistic with your expectations about what an individual can do, and in particular if they have a training requirement. You also need to be pragmatic about their time management and the amount of time they will have available to take on additional responsibility.

Will they, for example, need help to reorganise their own departments? Would it be appropriate to send them on a time management course? One of the best ways of making people feel responsible for their individual tasks is getting them to come up with timelines and goals for their own achievements. Rather than *telling* them what they should do, *asking* them what they think they could do is a much more effective way of getting their buy-in. The essence of getting buy-in into your plans is that your people feel accountable and responsible for the part they play in achieving the overall goal.

Buy-in from your customers

The next group of stakeholders who are worth communicating with are your customers. This is not conventionally what is done, but I think it's great to give them a sense of where you are trying to go with the business and what you are trying to achieve. Everyone likes to be associated with winners. If customers think you're a company that's going places, they will be more loyal to you. If you communicate well, you can generate a sense of excitement and community in the sense that they feel part of it as well.

Buy-in from your suppliers

Your suppliers shouldn't be neglected either, as they will have to grow with you in order for you to deliver to your customers. Making suppliers as valuable a part of your team as you do your own staff can be a hugely rewarding way of building up the business, while at the same time making sure you are not going to get left short by a supplier who is caught by surprise with your growth.

Don't forget your financial suppliers—the bank and potential investors in the business. They will want to see that you understand clearly what your business is about, that you have a strong sense of direction about where you are trying to go, and that your plan is both credible and achievable in terms of what you are setting out to do with the resources available.

MEASURING YOUR PLAN VERSUS THE REALITY

Those of us who have started a business know that plans are one thing and reality is entirely different. The unfortunate thing about business plans is that the only certainty that surrounds them is that they will be *wrong*! In other words, you may do better than you think or you may do worse than you think, but you won't, for sure, do *what* you think.

Bearing that in mind, you need to review and reassess the plan constantly in light of the reality of your situation. When I say 'constantly', I mean about once a month—you need to measure how your *plan* is doing against what you are *actually* doing, and then correct as you go along. Now as you get into the habit of having your monthly management meetings and, in particular, having a monthly report from the various departments of the business (with a financial update), you will be able to see quite clearly where the problem areas are.

DON'T BE TOO PROUD TO CHANGE

The essence of good business leadership is that you change when it is necessary, and you change again when it is necessary again, and you keep changing until you get it right. While you need to react to the events of the day and adjust, the idea of the business plan is that you have a clear sense of where you are going so that you can stay focused at the same time. So while you may get distracted by day-to-day events, the business plan will have articulated where it is you want to go in the long term. While you may have to change tack in the short term, it should be with a view to getting back to your long-term vision as soon as possible. Changing your plan as reality sets in involves lots of different things, from a greater sales effort, to a greater effort in reducing costs, to recognising that some people to whom you have allocated responsibility are not doing what they are supposed to be doing, either because they don't understand what they are supposed to be doing or because they are incapable of doing what they are supposed to be doing.

Change in one area of the business usually has implications in others. For example, a product that's not selling as well as intended will have a substantial effect on the revenue line in your business, on your sales and on your cash flow. That may result in needing to put more cash into the business than you anticipated when you originally compiled the plan.

Brody's 3 ideas on planning

- Go eat an elephant
- Don't be too proud to change
- Articulate your plan to your key stakeholders—staff and customers

Chapter 5
Innovating for Growth

When we started up in O'Briens back in 1988, our business model was essentially what it is today—to sell really good-quality sandwiches and coffee in an Irish-themed environment. Back then our coffee was brewed in one of those glass jugs on a hot plate and sold in polystyrene cups—and the coffee at the time, I think, sold for about 50p a cup.

The coffee was pretty good when it was freshly made, but unfortunately if it didn't sell fast, it deteriorated quite quickly. After about three hours it became undrinkable. We didn't sell very much of it—in fact it was a pretty insignificant part of our sales but, nevertheless, made up part of our top-line revenues.

Three or four years after starting the business, I read an article in a magazine about a new company called Starbucks which was based in Seattle on the west coast of America. Starbucks was revolutionising the way coffee was sold and was expanding rapidly across the US. Its system called for one cup of coffee, and one only, to be made at a time. I was intrigued. Together with our then design director, Steven Knight, I went off to America to visit Seattle and see what this company was all about.

After we arrived in Seattle and had checked into our hotel, we went for a walk in the downtown area. The first thing I noticed was people walking around sipping coffee out of large paper cups with funny plastic raised lids on the top. We noticed Starbucks stores everywhere: every street corner seemed to have one; every shopping mall; the entrance to every high-rise building. And in the Starbucks stores they were selling these tall paper cups with the funny raised lids.

I became really excited. I could see immediately the potential for doing the same thing in our fledgling O'Briens business back in Dublin. So we rushed back to Ireland, got rid of the old coffee machines from the six outlets, and found a supplier for these paper cups with the funny lids. The funny lids took a little while because nobody was doing them in Europe at the time. As we threw out all the old coffee machines, we replaced them with the latest espresso machines from Italy, which were used to make the new-style drinks, cappuccinos and lattes, then revolutionary new coffee products to Ireland. We put the new machines and new cups into the shops—and the results were dramatic.

The customers loved it, and they especially loved walking around with the paper cups and funny lids. In a very short period of time, coffee went from being 1–2 per cent of sales to 20 per cent. Instead of charging 50p a cup, we now charged €2. For what was essentially the same product, in the same cost cup, this was a dramatic improvement in the profit margin.

It had a further interesting effect. Prior to going down the cappuccino-to-go route, we were doing about 80 per cent of our business during the lunchtime period. But because we had at the time a unique and very attractive coffee offer, that 80 per cent went down to 50 per cent and, while we lost none of the cash revenue off the lunchtime business, the rest of the day expanded dramatically—particularly the early mornings and the afternoons. It was a truly defining innovation in our business. Yet when we think in terms of innovation, there is a tendency to think that it is all high-tech or high-falutin'. But essentially we just changed the way we were selling our coffee—and changed the way we packaged it—and it had a really dramatic effect.

The other point to note about our new coffee is that it was not our idea originally. We borrowed it from Starbucks, and because we were first to market with it in Ireland, we had a strong advantage over our competitors. Innovation doesn't have to be about inventing—to adapt an existing idea is much easier.

The point of this story, of course, is that small changes can have a very dramatic effect, and it was because of our openness to new ideas, and our constant quest to try and do things better, that we came across that particular one.

THE NUMBER 2 IDEA

Some people say that the secret of business success is having the Number 2 idea. At some point your Number 1 idea may run out of steam or be overtaken by some innovation of a competitor, and if you don't have a Number 2 idea, you are dead. A good example of this is the oft-quoted story of Ray Kroc, the person who built the McDonald's franchise. He started out life as a milkshake-machine salesman, and he went around the States selling his machines from which he derived commission.

On one of his sales tours he called in to see a new restaurant in San Bernardino, California, called McDonald's. This restaurant sold hamburgers and fries but also sold so many milkshakes that they had actually ordered eight machines. His interest was immediately aroused because initially he saw these McDonald's type of restaurants as fantastic users of his machines, and therefore his sales and his commission would be very high. But after a while he realised that the business model itself, of doing good-quality food in a kind of factory production-line environment, was the essence of the idea. Not long after that, he gave up selling milkshake machines (his Number 1 idea) and negotiated with the McDonald brothers for the rights to franchise the business across America. The rest is history.

Ray Kroc was open to having the Number 2 idea and, in fact, it was the Number 2 idea that ultimately led to his business success.

WHY IS INNOVATION IMPORTANT?

Aside from the stories we have just looked at, innovation is important because the world doesn't stand still.

The environment you are working in and selling in today is changing all the time as new technologies or new suppliers enter the industry. One of the downsides of great commercial success is that other people see what you are doing and try to imitate it. This is the case in our own business, where we had the gourmet sandwich and coffee market to ourselves for the first few years, but other entrepreneurs saw the perceived huge profits we were making and wanted a piece of the action.

You need to innovate as well, as your margins erode. This could be because of new entrants coming into the market who are willing to do things at a cheaper price or, as happened in Ireland, a minimum wage was introduced which increased our wage costs. And prices change, as happened recently where commodity prices (for example, wheat and dairy products) have shot through the roof.

We also need to innovate because customers' tastes change as people travel abroad more and their tastes become more sophisticated, but also as society itself changes. For example, the food industry has been defined for the last number of years by the concerns that some people have about obesity and healthy living.

This means you constantly need to refresh your offer, come up with Number 2 ideas, and try new things.

It is true to say that I am never satisfied by what we are doing and I think we can always do it *better*.

THINGS YOU CAN DO TO TURN YOURSELF INTO AN INNOVATOR

I would say that in my business career I never actually invented anything. What I did do, though, was take existing products or ways of doing things and try to figure out how to do them better. The coffee story quoted above is a good example of that. Improving what is already there is one of the easiest but also one of the best ways to innovate. It is an oft-quoted truism that pioneers are the ones who get shot, but it's the ones who follow after who make the money. Applying that to a business context, the person who invents something will often not make money out of it. The person who takes that idea and develops it is the one who does best financially out of it.

Good ideas are likely simply to happen

One day you are just walking along; out of the blue something comes to you; something strikes you about the way you are doing things and how you could do something better. The danger, of course, is that you might just forget it, as indeed you might if you get this brilliant brainwave in the middle of the night. For that reason it is a good idea to keep a notebook handy in your breast pocket or beside your bed. Get into the habit of writing things down as they occur to you. When you analyse it further, much of it will be gobbledegook, but there will be the occasional gem that you can actually put into action. Carrying a camera around with you for the same reason is a great idea, especially if you are looking at businesses similar to your own and it strikes you that something is being done particularly well.

You should be curious

Ask questions and be open to new ideas. I always like to talk to people to find out how things work, even if they are not directly related to my own business sphere. I think entrepreneurs are defined by curiosity and by not taking things at face value.

Read as much as you possibly can

Read not only about your own industry but about wider subjects. In Feargal Quinn's excellent book, *Crowning the Customer*, he wrote about his fresh-food counters where trained staff served customers. In particular, he described his butcher counters where customers went and interacted with a real butcher to get their meat cut or to get advice about how to cook it. For him this was one of the cornerstones that set him apart from his other supermarket competitors.

By listening to some of his customers, however, he realised that not all of his customers *wanted* to talk to a butcher. Some of them were looking for a much quicker and more convenient service, and indeed some of his customers didn't really like talking to people. On a trial basis in one of his stores he introduced pre-packaged meat in the refrigerated section, amid concern that it might take away from his existing butcher's counter and that, in fact, it could change customers' perception about his being a true fresh-food shop.

The trial proved to be a resounding success. He increased his meat sales without taking anything away from his butcher counters, and he had opened up a whole new facet of business he hadn't realised was there.

I used that story as the basis for changing how we sold our sandwiches, which initially were only sold on a made-to-order basis. I perceived, as Feargal Quinn did, that this was the essence of our business. On a trial basis and on the back of reading his story, we put in a pre-packaged sandwich counter with exactly the same results that he got. It took nothing away from the core business, but opened up an additional, profitable revenue flow.

The point is, I would never have found that out if I hadn't taken the trouble to read Quinn's book.

Try, try and keep trying

Most, in fact, nearly all the new ideas you try in your business will fail. Successful companies just keep at it. Supposing you get a new idea and you are convinced it will work; you try it and it doesn't work. What should you do? You could kill it, or perhaps change something about it and try again; and then change it and try again; and keep trying until you get it right.

Don't rely on gut instinct

You should do everything you can to get your brainwaves or ideas evaluated independently. Not long after starting O'Briens, we opened a new store in Baggot Street, the heart of the business district in Dublin. I had had the idea before we opened the new store that all existing sandwich bars, restaurants and cafés were really very dirty and gave customers a very poor perception of cleanliness.

I decided to decorate this new store in snow white throughout. It had white-tiled walls from floor to ceiling, white floors, white counters, staff were dressed in white coats—and so we opened it up. The problem was, it actually looked like a morgue, not a sandwich bar, and as a result customers didn't want to come anywhere near the place! Now if I had taken the trouble to talk that idea through with a few of my colleagues or friends before I did it, I am almost certain they would have put me off the idea, and I wouldn't have been so impetuous about doing it. It cost me an absolute fortune to change it and, of course, when I did change it back to a more normal-looking restaurant, sales took off and it became a great success.

Try to understand your preconceptions

I hate celery and so for years in our shops we never sold it. I have come to accept now that everybody doesn't think the way I do, and that some people in fact like celery—so we sell it now!

KAIZEN

You may have heard of the Japanese word 'kaizen'. *Kaizen* describes a process of continual improvement in a business and is often cited as one of the cornerstones of Japanese business success. Even though I hadn't heard of the term when we were starting our business, in fact we have a *kaizen* approach to running it. Today we have about 70 research and development projects on the go, from improving the way we write our operating manuals, to the way we merchandise the products in our stores, to improving the fillings in our sandwiches, to developing our corporate social responsibility strategy.

It has become part of our culture now to try constantly to do things better and, although a lot of our R&D projects run into a dead end, or in fact don't work, it is the principle of continuously trying that is important to us. Our mission statement is to be the best in the world at selling sandwiches and coffee. Clearly we are not the best in the world at selling sandwiches and coffee, but we won't have any hope of getting there unless we constantly try to improve every aspect of the business. I don't know about you, but I frequently look at our business and see that many things can be improved. You should consider your own business and how many aspects of it *you* are trying to improve at the moment, and maybe there are more that could be examined and improved. Eureka moments are rare. The founder of Sony is often quoted as saying that business success is 99 per cent failure and 1 per cent inspiration. Writing better operations manuals goes into the hard-work category; seeing how to sell coffee more successfully in paper cups with funny lids is maybe inspiration; but getting it on the shelves and in the shops is very hard work.

LISTEN TO STAFF AND CUSTOMERS

You should consider brainstorming new ideas or systems with your staff. It is an incredibly powerful way of figuring out how to do things better, and can be a great source of new ideas.

We sit down periodically with our staff and pose the questions: how can we do what we are doing better? Does anybody have new ideas for new products or services, or ideas on how we could save money? If you structure the brainstorm so that you record all the ideas (it doesn't matter how wacky they are) and have a process for sifting through them, evaluating them further and then taking the good ones out and making them happen, then you are well on the way to being an innovative company.

It is important to keep your new product development and ideas within your brand and vision ideals. So, for example, figuring out how to make a new type of chair may well be a good idea, but if it doesn't fit in with your vision of being the best in the world at selling sandwiches and coffee, then you don't really need to go down that road. That is why having a clear sense of vision for your business is so important. It means that as you consider these new ideas, you don't get distracted by them if they don't fit in with what you see as your core competencies.

The best ideas we have had in our business came from staff and customers who have said to us, 'You could do this better.'

WATCH THE COMPETITION—BUT NOT MORBIDLY!

Keeping an eye on the competition—and a close eye at that—is a pretty basic thing to do in any business. You are not watching them because you want to be second best or copy them directly, but because they are probably doing some aspects of their business better than you are.

In a business like ours, a retail business, we watch for things like speed of service—are they serving their food or handling their customers in a different way to the way we are? We look for unusual things that others are selling or offering as a service— perhaps they have got some bolt-on or add-on that we haven't figured out yet. We look for their prime selling space, to see if they have figured out which is the best selling space in the shop, what they are putting in there, and could we learn anything from that. We look to see if they are laying out their counters more effectively.

Human nature being what it is, we also look at how busy they are. Competitors always seem to be busier than you are! One of the sagest pieces of advice I received in my early years was not to mind how much money you thought your competitors were making, but to concentrate on your *own* game instead. That is a brilliant piece of advice, because wasting time with negative energy, worrying about why they seem to be doing it better, won't help to make your own business better. So I say, by all means watch the competition, but with the proviso that you should concentrate on your own game first.

Brody's 3 ideas on innovation

- It's easier to improve an existing product or service than to invent a new one
- Adopt the Japanese *kaizen* approach of continuous improvement
- Keep trying even when you're not having much success— it may be just around the corner

Chapter 6
Developing your Sales and Marketing Potential

I stood as a candidate for the Irish parliament, the Dáil, in 2007. From a marketing point of view, I had a very basic job to do—to sell myself to the electorate in my constituency. Two years prior to that I had commenced my campaign by canvassing door to door in all the houses in my area.

I remember well starting out, doing my first canvass, on my own in a housing estate on the north side of Dublin. I sat in my car, getting ready to go and knock on my first doors. Secretly, though, I was paralysed with nerves and fear. Here I was, a person who had received awards for selling, giving myself brown trousers at the prospect of getting out of the car to go and talk to an actual prospective customer. It was a salutary experience for someone who had lectured others—with some authority, I might add—on the benefits and ease of 'cold-calling'.

Over the course of two years, I knocked on the doors of the majority of the 26,000 houses in my constituency—twice. That's over 50,000 doors. Of these, I would say 99 per cent were pleasant, even if they had no intention of 'buying' off me. One per cent were downright nasty—but you could live with that. My preconceived fears about getting my head chewed off everywhere were totally wide of the mark, and I grew to enjoy canvassing and talking to people about their lives.

I ended this phase of my career with a much healthier respect than I had previously for people who work in sales, and particularly for people who cold-call for a living.

HOW TO BE SUCCESSFUL IN SALES

There is only one way to be successful in business and that is to sell your products profitably. Whatever your product is, that is all there is to it, yet half of us struggle with it. For many businesses trying to grow from small to tall, scaling up their sales will be one of the biggest challenges. As we try to do so, and if it's a struggle, we tend to blame the product or the sales material, when what really may be wrong is the *way* we are doing it. Too often we think the product has some intrinsic flaw—it is too expensive, too big, too small—but maybe we just haven't found the correct way to package the product for the sort of customers who might like to buy it. Let's look at some of the elements that go into getting your products sold.

You

Companies that are successful at selling are run by people who will do whatever it takes to get the products sold. Doing whatever it takes means, when your sales methods don't work for some reason, or don't work often enough or quickly enough, that you change them, and you change them again and again until you get them right. At this stage of your organisation's life, you may be the only one who can do that.

Selling your products may involve you doing some things that you are not comfortable with, like cold-calling. But if you are absolutely serious about building your business and building your sales, then you have got to do whatever it takes.

Many sales campaigns don't work the way they are intended to, not because they are wrong but because they are badly executed. Figuring out in which way they were badly executed and then changing the campaign so that you don't do it in that way again, seems obvious, but if you're not relentlessly focused on getting it right, then you will probably repeat the mistake, but in a different way. So, to reiterate, successful sales is about doing whatever it takes: adjusting and adjusting again and again, and doing stuff sometimes that you don't like doing.

The people who sell with you

When I was involved in my political campaigning, asking people to vote for me, I had many canvassers who came out to support me by knocking on doors with me. It became apparent to me, however, that despite the generosity and goodwill of so many supporters who knocked on doors and introduced me to people, some of them were just not suited to it and were actually putting *off* potential voters. Some were a little too strident in their views; others didn't have great interpersonal skills, and so were unable to establish a rapport with a voter and were therefore unlikely to persuade them to vote in a particular way.

Before doing anything else with your salespeople, you should reassess them as people. Are they the right people for the job? Are they extroverted? Most salespeople are. Or are they quiet mice who prefer their own company? Do you need to make changes in this area?

This may also be true in the actual sales of your product, and you need to recognise that somebody with poor interpersonal skills, for example, is unlikely to make a great salesman. Most sales campaigns that are successful are successful because of the hard work of a sales team, and salespeople make up the sales team. Good sales come from people who are happy in their work, and as we will see in the Managing Your People section, people who are happy in their work respond to having a vision of where the business is supposed to be going. They need to be properly trained, to get a pat on the back when they are doing well, to get a shoulder to lean on when they are not, to have clear targets and goals and to get regular feedback as to how they are doing. None of this is rocket science. Yet we seem to spend all our time on sales techniques with our sales staff rather than making sure their attitude is right. Salespeople aren't parrots.

KNOWING YOUR CUSTOMERS—LOW-LEVEL MARKET RESEARCH

Knowing who your customers are and where they come from means you can tailor your products to suit them. Knowing what turns them on and off, and knowing what they really think of you and your products, are key to successful selling. There are lots of ways of getting to know your customers, but one of the easiest is by doing some low-level market research—low-level in the sense that you can do a lot of it yourself, and you don't need to hire an expensive market research company to do it for you. Talk to your customers on the shop floor. Take the trouble to ring your customers after you have made a sale to ask them what they thought of the sales process, what they now think of the product and its value, and how they think you can improve.

I notice my partner Lulu doing just this after Christmas each year. She phones around the clients who have ordered Christmas hampers from her company, 4Giftsdirect.com, to ask if they were happy with the service. As well as getting useful feedback, she is 'under-promising and over-delivering'. Her customers do not expect a call in January to find out if they were happy, so they will think better of her and her company when they go to make their orders again next year. This common-sense approach to listening is often ignored in favour of big technical studies which often don't catch the feel of what your relationship with your customer is like.

Low-level market research doesn't cost much to do, and is often substantially more accurate than research compiled and carried out by people who don't know your business terribly well. If you have the money, you can of course employ a professional market research agency, but it is worth being careful about the type of decisions you make on foot of market research results. Let me give you an example.

There was an article recently in one of our restaurant trade magazines about the Wendy's hamburger chain in the US. In America, Wendy's is the number three hamburger chain after McDonald's and Burger King. Some years ago they carried out research to find out what type of food Wendy's customers wanted them to serve. Now this was at the height of obesity awareness, mad cow disease and other scares about eating red meat, so, not surprisingly, their customers responded by saying, for example, that they wanted to see more salads on the menu, less deep-fried food, more healthy options and smaller portions. On foot of this research, Wendy's introduced a salad range; they took away their largest hamburger; they had less deep-fried food; they had more healthy options—and their sales *didn't* improve! In fact, for the two or three years that they ran with this menu on foot of this customer research, their sales continued to decline. At the end of the period in question, they started to do away with their cold sandwich options and their salads (or at least to put lesser emphasis on them). Strangely, their sales began to climb again, and eventually they went back to pretty much the menu they had before the exercise—and the sales showed quite healthy increases.

The point of this story is that market research told them a story that wasn't really true and, in fact, Wendy's came to the conclusion that the customers had lied, not deliberately, but nevertheless they had lied—lied in the sense that what they had told Wendy's was what their aspirations were in terms of eating. Yes, they would *like* to eat more healthy food, they would *like* to eat smaller portions, and they would *like* to eat more salads— but they didn't want to do it *today*! It was an aspiration that was for some indeterminate time in the future. Today, they were going to have their super-sized meal with their large Coke, but maybe the day after, they would think about it. So you need to be careful when you do your market research, to ask the right questions in order to hear the right answers.

SOURCE THE CUSTOMERS

Customers for your products can come from an almost infinite number of sources. Some are obvious, some not so, but it is worth considering the most important ones and here is a list of some of them:

Existing customers—in other words, customers already buying from you. These are the most important but often the most neglected group.

'Not todays'—customers who won't make a purchasing decision today, but may do so at another stage.

Past enquiries—people who have enquired about your product or service before but then didn't quite follow it up.

Follow your customers—if one of your customers moves to a new job, you can contact them when they are in place at their new job, as well as getting introduced to the person taking over from them in their old one.

Lapsed customers—there is an old saying, 'Once a customer, always a customer.' Just because somebody hasn't bought from you recently doesn't mean they are never going to buy from you ever again.

Location—in retail and indeed in most businesses, of course, location is the most important source of new customers.

Advertising—in whatever medium, advertising can provide a great source for new customers. They say in advertising that 50 per cent of your budget is wasted—the trouble is you never know which 50 per cent it is. It is also expensive and costs a lot more money for lead generators than perhaps a lot of other sources.

Sampling—to let the potential customer try a sample free or at a very reduced cost is a great way of generating leads.

Cold-calling—despite all our advances in technology, cold-calling is as popular a way as ever of generating sales appointments.

Referrals/introductions—these are among the most effective ways to source new customers.

Unprompted word of mouth—the holy grail of sales.

PR—creating good news stories about your business which stimulate customers to purchase from you.

Newspaper ads—an unusual source of leads for customers for the business but nevertheless a potentially valuable one. For example, advertisements or planning notices can provide great leads for builders or landscape gardeners because there are clear intentions to develop a piece of property.

BEST CUSTOMERS ARE EXISTING CUSTOMERS

The Automobile Association (AA) used to drive me mad. As a long-standing customer, paying my bill conscientiously each time by direct debit, I would pass one of their salesmen in a booth at a shopping mall, offering potential new customers a 40 per cent discount on what regular members were being charged. I'm sorry, but I found that offensive. They didn't appear to care about their loyal existing customers and were interested only in getting new ones. Halifax were recently offering a free €100 if you open a credit card account with them. Does this apply to their loyal existing customers? Not a chance!

It is all too easy when talking about selling to concentrate almost exclusively on new customer acquisition, yet the customers that are the absolute best, and the bedrock of your business, are in fact your existing customers.

They know you. By definition they like you, otherwise they wouldn't be doing business with you, and they don't need to be educated at great expense about your product or service. Yet we tend to ignore them and concentrate only on getting new ones. The question should be: how can we sell more to our existing customers, because, in fact, these are the easiest extra sales we are ever going to get into the business.

The best way to keep track of who your existing customers are, what they are buying and what their preferences are, is by having a really good database. This should contain not only their basic contact information but also their preferences in terms of the product or service, frequency of purchase and even personal details, so that you can congratulate them on some personal achievement.

In sales, not nearly enough importance is attached to the database, both of existing customers and of prospects which are correctly analysed, so that you know when it is time to go after them again. The database is the absolute treasure for a sales business.

WORKING OUT THE PROCESS—KNOWING YOUR SALES FORMULA

There is a formula that lots of businesses have found really effective in terms of understanding how their sales work:

Winning product + Good sales formula = Great sales

On the basis that you already have your winning product, how can you find a formula that will deliver sales to you—a formula, the workings of which you can understand?

For most organisations there will be a tried and tested method of getting the sale, or raising the funds, or achieving the business objective. Even if your organisation is young, that formula is probably there; it's just that you may not have realised it yet. If you find out what your formula is, it can help you plan and budget your sales effort, and direct your sales staff clearly as to how to achieve your plans. Your formulas could contain a people element or a simple process element. For example,

So many cold-calls = so many sales
(it's the people's effort involved)

2" x 6" ad in the *Sunday Times* = x enquiries per product
(that is process)

Knowing your formula intellectually is one thing; actually making sure to implement it is another. Let us look at a formula in our business for making a franchise sale, which I think will demonstrate this point to you.

We have found from experience over the years that to sell a franchise we need, on average, to generate 100 enquiries, which will lead to five people sending application forms in, of whom four will come for an interview, and one will end up buying. Or to put it more simply,

100 brochures mailed ⇨ 5 applications ⇨ 4 interviews = 1 sale

Of course there are many other factors involved in persuading someone to buy one of our franchises; sending 100 brochures out when the fundamentals of the business are wrong just won't work. But from a sales perspective alone it is a useful measure.

This means that to sell 10 franchises in a year, we need to generate 1,000 enquiries, so generating 1,000 enquiries becomes the sales objective for which 10 sales are ultimately made. We know that, all things being equal, if we can generate only 600 enquiries in a year, we will not achieve our objective of selling 10 franchises.

You know the formula, but it's not happening

Having a formula is one thing, but making it work is another. If it has worked in the past, but isn't any more, you need to start asking yourself some questions:

- Have the sales personnel changed; are they doing their job properly?
- Has the external environment changed? Higher interest rates, economic uncertainty and strong competition are some of the factors which affect your formulas.
- Is your product up to scratch or has it deteriorated? Is there some fundamental flaw with it that you haven't twigged yet?

Having the correct attitude is the most important ingredient in sales success—that and having the desire to be successful. It is not just somebody's ability that makes that success happen. Let's look at some of the reasons why sales don't grow.

An existing customer is not buying enough

This can stem from the actual orders being too small or simply not getting enough repeat business. It is worth doing some low-level market research to find out what the root cause is. It may simply be that we are not actually trying to sell more to existing customers because we're so busy trying to get new ones.

Customers buying from competitors

Of course, customers or non-customers have for years been buying, and will continue to buy, from competitors, often just because they have established a close relationship with a supplier or because the competitor is meeting their need.

While it can be difficult to break that relationship, it's not impossible; it is a question of being relentless and consistent in keeping after it, even when you are being rejected.

Not doing enough prospecting

Not doing enough prospecting means you're not generating enough leads, which means you're not getting enough sales appointments. This goes right back to understanding your formula and what you need to do—i.e. prospecting.

INSTANT TIPS

There are many, many books written about sales which offer advice and help as to how to do it better. This book can't hope to cover the subject in any great detail, but some of the things I have found particularly useful in trying to sell to customers in my business life are as follows:

Ask for advice

If you are trying to get in to see a potential customer for your business, often they won't respond well to a direct sales approach. However, if you use the pretext of asking them for advice, they may respond much better to this approach. It's because asking for advice appeals to the ego and good nature of the person being asked—especially men's.

The AIDA approach

(Attention, Interest, Desire, Action)—AIDA is a common acronym I have been using for years to help design promotional literature and, in particular, leaflets. It is not my own invention but one I have found useful to keep in mind when I am thinking about designing something. A good piece of promotional literature should contain each of the AIDA elements in the correct sequence. For example, the first thing you need to do with promotional material is capture somebody's attention. That means the reader has to be willing to give the piece of literature more than a second glance. This demands that the headline on the front of the piece of literature, or the colour, or the graphics used, has to really grab somebody's attention. After you have got their attention you have now to stimulate their interest by telling them about the product or service you are selling. The 'interest' bit has to be described in a simple way that makes potential customers want to find out more. The third thing you need to do is stimulate desire, and desire is stimulated by selling not the product but the benefits of the product. For example, if I was selling a weight loss product I might write, 'Become confident and sexy by using x product.' The last part of AIDA is 'action', or, specifically, a call to action. You need to stimulate your potential customers to make a purchasing decision, and perhaps that is by offering money off or an extra free gift if a customer orders by a specific date.

The person who aims high will get more

With a lot of products you sell, customers buy them infrequently. Products like a car, a carpet, getting the house painted or getting grinds for students, are all things that potential customers may not be totally familiar with in terms of their value. In other words, you don't really know how the customer values something. For example, you may sell a product on price when the customer's principal issue is security, for which they are prepared to pay almost any price. The point here is that we often under-sell ourselves by thinking only in terms of price, instead of thinking of the benefits that customers might get. If we think in terms of benefits first, often we will adjust our price accordingly.

Think carefully before you discount

It is very tempting, when you are trying to build the sales of a product, to offer discounts to customers. But for the same reasons mentioned above, maybe the customer has a different perception of the value. When we were selling our franchises in the early days, I made it an absolute policy that we wouldn't discount to the franchisee. This was for a couple of reasons: one was because I believed we had greater integrity with the business if we didn't discount and we stuck to our guns. The second reason was just as important: that our existing franchisees didn't get annoyed or upset because they found that we had sold a franchise at a reduced price to somebody else.

Use handwritten letters

Sadly, the art of handwriting has become rare in modern life. In fact, I have noticed that when I do get a handwritten letter, I give it a lot more attention than I would a typed one. This can be a great advantage when you are trying to sell something, in particular, if you are trying to get in to see somebody very senior in a company that you would like to have as your customer. By sending a handwritten letter you are demonstrating that you think they are important enough to take the trouble to actually sit down and write a letter to them. It is generally well received, and you are much more likely to get a personal response than to be fobbed off.

People don't spend money; they buy value

This goes back to the point I made earlier in this section about how people who aim high get more. Customers aren't always thinking about the price; they are much more concerned that they get value, and value is something that means different things to different people.

Recognise your customers' achievements

Any opportunity to cement your relationship with your customer, over and above your commercial relationship, should be taken very seriously. Often you will spot something complimentary about your customers in a newspaper or hear about it on the radio, and it is well worthwhile to send a handwritten note congratulating them or noticing the fact. Customers are the same as people working for you. They appreciate recognition.

Brody's 3 ideas for selling

- Get to know your sales formula
- Be prepared to do whatever it takes
- Make sure you have the right people in the job

Chapter 7
Financing your Growth

GETTING THE INVESTMENT REQUIRED TO GROW THE BUSINESS

Some 15 years ago now, when my fledgling business had grown to three stores, I approached some venture capital companies with a view to getting them to invest in the business and help me expand. To say that they wouldn't treat me seriously was an understatement, and I was sent packing with my tail between my legs, chastened by the way they had reacted to my audacity.

When we had 30 stores some years later, the same venture capital company approached me. As the same company who had turned me down all those years ago now pleaded for an opportunity to provide finance for us, I carefully examined the back of my hands as I mulled over their proposition. It was very tempting for me to say no, but we needed the money and we needed it there and then, so we took our first serious investment into the business, and to be truthful we never looked back.

In this chapter we look at all the elements around financing the growth of your business. So we're going to look at things like

- What you really need the finance for
- What the business is worth right now—really important
- Is the business capable of getting funds?
- How much of the business to consider selling
- Sources of finance
- Some of the issues around taking in outside capital and outside investors.

WHAT YOU REALLY NEED THE FINANCE FOR

So let's start by looking at what you need the finance for, and that's a good opportunity to have a really honest appraisal about where you are. Just because you're growing doesn't mean you need a Rolls Royce approach—it's not a perfect world. If you got by this far by driving a beat-up old van, renting a second-rate premises and paying yourself peanuts, it doesn't mean that just because you're now looking for some serious investment to move the business on to the next stage, you need to drive a flash car, have superb offices and pay yourself a king's ransom. In other words, you don't need to totally change overnight the way you're doing things.

Usually the first thing we need finance for is to satisfy our day-to-day cash flow requirements. In particular, if your business is growing rapidly, it's usually short of working capital. As you look at what you need finance for (and include your drawings in that), be realistic about them and try to anticipate what the growth of your business is going to mean in terms of your cash requirement.

Often the second thing we need as we look to get outside investment into the business is an amount of money to satisfy what I call legacy debt. Legacy debt is basically the cash that you've used up, probably in losses while you got the business off the ground. That legacy debt will usually be in the form of an unhealthy balance of your trade creditors, bank loans and indeed personal loans that you, or someone close to you, has put into the business. Raising new finance for the business is an opportunity to deal with these and get that monkey off your back.

The next thing you might look at getting financing for is to buy out some existing shareholders in the business, who for whatever reason may want to exit or, indeed, you may want to get them out. But you must ask yourself the question: is this the right time to do it or would I be better hanging on until later?

You may also look at raising finance to purchase your premises, and while that may be a good idea, it's worth thinking about what business you're in. Most of us who are not directly involved in property development are not in the property business, so you have to question whether that's the best use of your money. Not having to buy your premises obviously substantially reduces the funds you're trying to raise.

You may also want to raise finance to invest in developing the business, and that's a good time to ask questions about what you're proposing to do—whether, for instance, you're developing it around the existing model or want to go off into new areas. Let me give you an example about that.

I had a couple of guys referred to me by one of my banking friends. They were looking to raise about €1.5 million for their business. They were franchisees of a large retail franchisor, and they were looking to buy out the master licensee for Ireland. They had decided as part of this buy-out that they would set up a warehouse to service the existing franchisees in the business. At that time there were about 40 of those in existence, and they thought they could provide a much more efficient service than the incumbent master franchisee by having said warehouse, and hence the need for €1.5 million development capital.

When I went through the business plan with them, it became clear to me that operating this warehouse was not a key part of their business model. Like ourselves in O'Briens, the important aspect of their becoming the master franchisees was the direct support they gave to their operators, and the marketing and technical support they provided to back them up. The idea of a warehouse was actually well down the list of priorities. When we got into it in detail, it transpired that the warehouse was costing about €800,000 to set up, and when we eliminated that from the business model, it meant that in fact they were looking for about €700,000 of development capital, and not €1.5 million.

I spent an hour with these guys and they almost kissed me on the way out because, not only had I radically changed their perception of how the business was going to operate but, equally importantly, I had essentially halved the capital requirement they were looking for, and of course that was much easier to raise.

What we have looked at are some of the reasons you may want to raise money—there may be others that I haven't covered. The point of this section is to make you think through carefully what you want the money for, and whether it's the right time to go and get it.

WHAT'S THE BUSINESS WORTH?

Let us look next at what the business might be worth right now. The perceived value depends, of course, on whether you're a buyer or a seller. For example, if you're selling shares in the business, you want to get the value up as high as you can and maximise the return to yourself as the shareholder.

If, however, you are in the position of buying out an existing shareholder, for example, it would suit you much more to have the value of the business really low—absolutely rock bottom— because if you are a buyer, you want to buy as cheaply as you can.

So you could have the same company with two completely different perceptions of the value from your point of view, depending on whether you're a seller or a buyer.

We recently had a situation in our business where our venture capital company, who had supported us so well over the years, wanted to cash in on their investment. Now this was perfectly normal and understandable from their point of view, in that they had left their investment in the business for seven years. The investment fund through which they had made the investment was winding up, and they wanted to realise the asset.

At the time they held 20 per cent of the business, and when we intimated to them that we would be interested in buying in the stake, they gave us a figure that they thought it was worth. Now in truth when we heard the figure they were looking for, we thought it was pretty good value. The venture capital company was getting a very good return on the money they had invested, but, from our point of view, we felt they had significantly undervalued the business, and so we were very keen to try and buy in the stake.

However, as you do, we went back to the venture capital company and said that they were ridiculously over-valuing the business, and it was worth substantially less than that. In fact we negotiated a lower price with them, to a level where we thought it really was cheap. As I say, the venture capital company were getting a good return for their investment, so they were happy to get out at the figure.

After a long period of negotiation we did a deal with the venture capital company and raised the funds to buy out the 20 per cent stake, and indeed did just that. No sooner had we bought in the stake than we had an approach from a trade investor to buy a substantial stake in the business. Our opening position was at a figure three times the value that had been used to buy out our venture capital partners. The point of telling this story is, what sort of value you're going to put on the business depends greatly on whether you're a seller or a buyer.

Having said that, here are a couple of pointers on how you might value your business right now. Firstly, if you're a relatively new high-growth business, you get a much better valuation by selling on blue sky than on reality. By that I mean that when you sell, you get a much better value for your business based on its future growth prospects rather than its historical earnings. The fact that a new high-growth company does not have historical earnings is quite understandable and acceptable to an outside investor, who will look for the growth that a good executive team may bring to it. If your company was, however, long established with limited growth prospects, then you are much more likely to be valued on your historical earnings, and that is likely to be a lower valuation than you would get if it was on future high growth.

If you are selling on historical earnings, you are really selling on a track record of your profitability, and usually businesses are valued on what is known as a p-e ratio (or price-earnings ratio).

What that means is that your business is worth a multiple of the annual profits before you take off interest, depreciation and drawings. So, for example, if your business had been making an average profit of €500,000 a year for the last three years, and was pretty stuck in its ways, somebody who was looking to buy into that business might value it at seven or eight times its annual earnings—in other words, eight times €500,000 which would be €4 million. This is the p-e ratio where the price p (€4 million) is eight times the annual profit e (€500,000). Depending on the investor's appetite for your type of business, or indeed for the business sector, that p-e ratio might go up or down. So, for example, this year a lot of our big, long-established institutional banks have been trading on p-e ratios of eight or nine, whereas what are perceived as high-growth companies like internet gambling companies are getting p-e ratios of 30 or 40. Obviously this creates a completely different value for the business.

In order to try and have a stab at a valuation for your business, you would start by preparing projections for up to five years out, and seeing what they looked like.

An investor will then discount that five years' profitability to allow for the high risk involved, and place a valuation on it which may or may not be in the ballpark of what you are looking for.

Valuing a business is a highly complex process, where decisions are often made on an emotional basis rather than a factual one. A good example of that was the dot-com boom some years ago. There was no historical basis for saying these dot-com businesses were going to be successful, but people got caught up in the hysteria around them, and the most unlikely founders of companies got funded and then sold out—and made a fortune—long before the investors woke up to the fact that they were worthless.

IS THE BUSINESS CAPABLE OF RAISING THE FUNDS?

Let's look now at whether the business is capable of getting the funds. Now *you* might think your business is worth some money, but will anyone else?

At the end of the day your business is worth what someone is willing to pay for it, and it is likely that they will back you first and your business second. This is where knowing what you really want financially is so important because, for instance, your business may not be capable of raising €5 million in development capital now, but could be capable of raising €2.5 million. So if you go in looking for €5 million and cannot get it, you may have ruined your prospects of getting €2.5 million, because you have now made your potential investors negative on the business. I have seen people shoot too high, too quickly, too many times, trying to get the business funded. There was nothing wrong with the business and nothing wrong with the founder, but they just went too quickly and were too ambitious, and didn't understand what investors would be looking for.

HOW MUCH OF THE BUSINESS SHOULD YOU CONSIDER SELLING?

The next thing to consider is how much of the business to consider selling. Some people are very funny about selling a share in their business. They want to hold on to everything, partly because they like the idea of keeping all the profits, but probably more importantly because they like the idea of keeping all of the control.

I have long been of the view that I would prefer to own 10 per cent of a really successful company which was worth a lot of money than 100 per cent of a company whose control or financial equity I wasn't willing to surrender. In other words, 10 per cent of something is worth a lot more than 100 per cent of nothing. When you think about selling shares in a business, you should be doing it as part of a strategy, and that comes back to your vision of what the business should be like in the future. So, for example, you may look at taking some capital in now which would carry you through the next phase of your growth, on the basis that you take in a really large amount of capital in three or four years to really scale up the business then. A lot of companies do this and it is known as first-round, second-round, third-round funding. The point in thinking this strategy through before you go after the first lot is that you do not want to give away too much of the equity too early on, when the value of the business is likely to be low, but you do need to give enough away to make it attractive to an outside investor.

This is one of the areas where it's important to get outside advice from either your accountant or corporate finance advisers.

SOURCES OF FINANCE

Let us now look at some sources of finance. Before we start, it is a good idea to consult with your advisers again before you set yourself out on the road. Probably the most important adviser you have in those early stages of the business is your accountant, especially if he/she is a good one.

My first serious accountant was Dominic Kelly. When we were mulling over the proposed first investment from our venture capital company, it was he who suggested we go for a valuation of €5 million for the business. I frankly didn't think it was worth that, but he encouraged me to shoot for the stars and not to under-sell myself. He was right, and the first investment was made at that level. I would never have got that on my own.

Your accountant should have a good general picture about both what you are trying to do and your likelihood of success. He will also have a good idea of how to go about it, and of course he will help you prepare the all-important business plan. While he should and may help you prepare the business plan, you should do most of the work on it yourself so that you understand what it is you are putting down on paper.

One of the things that is often overlooked when you decide to get money into the business is the amount of time and effort that is required to do so. You will be involved in meetings with advisers and potential investors; you will be involved in business plans and financial projections for the business; you may have to tidy up the business to make it more attractive to an outside investor—all these things take a considerable amount of time and effort. The problem is that you may spend so much time and effort on trying to get new finance in that you actually take your eye off the ball of the core business itself. Maybe you are not watching your margins as closely as you should, or you are not getting in the sales calls that you should be doing, or you're not spending the time with your customers that you normally would. So it is worth considering, as you go off and look at the various sources of finance—what if you have made all this effort and you just cannot get the money at the moment? Will all the effort and time you have taken off from the business jeopardise the existing business? Indeed, the size of the fees that you may now have to pay an accountant or corporate finance adviser may threaten the very existence of the business itself.

Banks

Let us start with banks. Your bank will probably be the first call you make when you are looking for funds for the business, and in truth they may be your best chance—in the sense that they have an existing relationship with you and they know you a bit.

I have always found it a good idea to send my accountant in for an informal chat with my bank manager before I go in myself. The idea behind this is that your accountant can pick up informally how the bank manager is likely to react to a proposal before you suffer the ignominy of a formal refusal.

In my book, *Making Bread*, we looked at the fact that banks are not supposed to take risks with customers' money. It is worth recounting a story that my bank manager told me which helps explain why so many propositions get turned down. He told me that he had never in his career at the bank seen a business plan presented to him that didn't show the bank being repaid in full and on time. He had never seen one, and yet, as he explained, approximately 90 per cent of the business plans that were presented to him did require adjustment—not always negatively, he said, but the point was he knew that what was written down was not likely to happen.

Business angels
Business angels are private investors whom you contact informally and who may have an interest in investing in your business. They can be a great addition to your business because not only can they provide you with funds, but they may also choose to get involved as a director of your business, and mentor and coach you as you go about trying to build it up. This is because, of course, they have a significant financial interest in how the business develops. There are established ways of trying to get business angels interested in your business. There are investment clubs and ways whereby you can find out about getting to these people.

A good tip is to find one who is interested in your area. So, for example, you may find one who is very strong on technology companies but has absolutely no interest in retail.

Venture capital companies
Venture capital companies are ideally placed to provide the development capital you need to grow the business. They have also been around the block, are used to high risk, and will give you an honest appraisal of what they see as your plans and your prospects.

We have had very positive experiences with our venture capital investors. They got involved with us when we were producing our plans. Having approved them, they basically let us get on with it. They bring financial discipline to the business because you have to produce management accounts for them. In our case they also appointed a director to the board and that also brought a discipline into our board meetings. The only times when they expressed concern or got involved was when we were clearly going outside our plans—where we went off our stated aims. As I say, all in all a good experience for us.

As with business angels, it is worth doing a bit of research on the various venture capital companies out there to find one that is interested in your sector. I also think it is worth approaching two or three at the same time on the basis that two of them are likely to say no, and you have not wasted a large amount of time in the process waiting around for somebody to make up their mind.

Corporate financiers

Corporate financiers, who may work for one of the big stock-broking firms, are another way of trying to get finance into your business. A corporate financier may introduce you to a venture capital company, or indeed private high-net-worth clients of the brokerage. My advice is to be very careful choosing one of them, because once you are in bed with them it is very difficult to get out.

They will be motivated to get a good value for the business because usually it is on a percentage basis of the funds raised that they will be paid. They may be motivated beyond what is sensible for you, when on reflection it might be better for you to take a step back and rethink your investor strategy, and perhaps try and go for a different investor or a different type of investor.

I think it is worth getting some help from a mentor or adviser before you go in to see a corporate financier, and in particular when you are negotiating a fee with them.

Family

When you have exhausted every other possibility of getting finance, family are often the only ones left to turn to, and the only ones with any reason to support you.

It is worth thinking really carefully about the implications of getting your family involved in the business, and in particular the effect it may have on your family relationships. There is nothing like money to wreck a close family relationship.

If you do end up receiving funding to develop the business by someone in your family, you should treat it in as businesslike a manner as you possibly can, and make formal, written agreements about when the money is to be repaid and in what way. As importantly, you should agree about what is to happen if the repayment terms are not met. Because it is family, you can always renegotiate these at the appropriate time, but at least you are starting on a clean and professional basis where everybody's expectations can be dealt with at the time.

Taking a partner in

Taking a partner in could also be one of the only avenues open to you financially, where you would be aiming to take somebody into the business who has complementary skills to your own.

I think one of the first things you should consider when thinking about taking in a partner is that if you did not actually need the money, would you take them in? To my mind, that's the acid test of whether or not you would be in a partnership with somebody. And if you do think it's a good idea to take somebody in as a partner, would they be better as an active partner or as a silent partner? It's a truism that, for many partnerships, the reasons people thought they were going into the partnership before they commenced it, changed once the partnership commenced. And while that may change in a very positive way (and often does), you should also be conscious that it could change in a way that is negative.

It is absolutely essential when you look at partnerships, or indeed taking family in, that you sign what is effectively a pre-nuptial agreement. This is an agreement where you ask all the awkward what-if questions that involve subjects like 'trust'.

So, for example, what if one of you wants to sell your share in the business; what if the business needs more money invested in it; what if one of you gets sick and the other one is doing all the work? Asking these questions *before* the partnership commences means they are much less likely to be an issue as the partnership develops. You should include also in those questions the expectations of what work each partner is going to do.

Trade (suppliers)

Trade investors are an often overlooked source of development funding for your business. By that I mean suppliers who are doing good business with you. They can see how your business is growing and may well feel in a position, from their own point of view, to support you financially. They may do this by either actually investing cash in the business or by extending you credit lines. Unlike many other potential investors, they can actually see the level of business you are doing, the growth you are achieving and how you conduct your business affairs. They may feel very strongly that you are worth backing in a way that other investors would not know about.

The potential difficulty with a trade investor coming into the business is that often it locks out other potential avenues of investment for the business. For example, if one of your suppliers came in and took a 20 per cent share in the business, it means you would almost be precluded from approaching one of your other suppliers, or other potential new suppliers, for investment in the business because you have this one on board.

IPO (initial public offering)

IPOs are something to consider as you develop the business, but it is way beyond the scope of this book as to whether they are a good thing or a bad thing for your business. An IPO is something you would consult your financial adviser about, and potentially your corporate finance advisers, to help you decide if it was the right thing for your business at this particular time.

Some of the things worth considering about IPOs are: firstly, the reporting requirements for public companies can be very onerous, and your adviser's fees/corporate finance fees would be high. When you put that against the amount of money you could potentially raise, is it worth it? The second point to make is that your company's performance becomes very public, as it is reported on frequently in the financial press.

Development agencies

Development agencies like county and city enterprise boards and industrial development agencies may well consider investing in your business as part of a bigger investment package. In other words, if you can attract some initial investment, they may well come along and provide the balance that you are looking for.

In addition, they may provide some employment, training grants or subsidies, premises, or grants towards attending foreign trade shows.

ISSUES AROUND TAKING MONEY IN

Finally let us take a look at some of the issues around taking capital into the business.

First of all, there is the cost of raising the funds and for a small business this can often be a substantial amount of money. As I mentioned earlier, it is worth thinking about, particularly if the fundraising exercise has to be aborted for any reason or you just cannot get it. I think that is why it is worth going through the exercise above with your accountant before committing yourself to any particular avenue.

Some of the costs you are likely to incur in raising your capital will include corporate finance fees and fees paid to your accountant—for work done on the business plan, perhaps on tax advice, general advice fees, and for helping you prepare a prospectus. You may have to pay fees to your lawyers, and when you fundraise, for example, from a venture capital company, not only will you be expected to pay lawyers' fees—and they may charge you an arrangement fee for actually setting up an investment—but of course your bank may also charge you an arrangement fee for any funds they put in place for you.

Shareholders' agreements

If you are involved in taking in outside investment, for example, from a venture capital company or business angel or indeed a development agency, you are going to have to sign a shareholders' agreement with them. Some of the things you might want to consider in a shareholders' agreement would include:

- Whether or not there will be a director appointed to represent the investor, which could be the investor himself or an executive from the venture capital company.
- When you might want to sell the shares or the investor might want to sell his shares and what are known as pre-emption rights. This means that you agree before you enter into the arrangement with the investor under what circumstances either of you may sell your shares, and usually that you will have to offer your shares to the other investor on the same terms as you may have negotiated with a third party.
- Next, the investors may want to lock in the founders of the business and preclude the founder of the business from selling any of his shares before the investors sell theirs.
- You will be obliged to make regular management reports as part of a shareholders' agreement.
- Establish what your dividends policy will be; in truth, dividends are not usual in a high-growth company.
- You will be obliged to declare your true profitability—which may or may not suit you at the time. In other words, you lose the flexibility of shifting some of your profit or loss into the preceding or following years for tax purposes.

You should think about the investment as being made up entirely or partly of preference shares which usually don't carry voting rights but do have interest payable. Many venture capital companies will want to invest in your business on a mixture basis (a mixture of ordinary shares and preference shares).

Finally, when you get the money, celebrate. It is a great, great moment, but remember that getting the money is not the business objective—it is only a step on the journey.

Brody's 3 ideas on fundraising

- Decide how much you need, then go back and decide what the amount is, so that you have to surrender only the smallest amount of equity
- 5 per cent of something valuable is worth a lot more than 100 per cent of nothing
- Sell on hope and blue sky, not on reality

Chapter 8
Managing your Money

I know as I was growing my business I had very little interest in the financial management of it. In fact, managing my money turned me cold, and in the very early years, I ran my finances by the age-old black sack method. I used to collect my paperwork at the end of every month and throw it into the aforementioned black sack, leaving it for my accountant to sort out. This, naturally, was not a healthy way to run my finances, but it reflected the importance I gave it at that time and my own horror at the thought of the boredom I would endure by having to sit down and deal with all those figures. Of course, my accountant also had to change me—more to sort out the mess— at a time when I could least afford it.

In this chapter we will re-examine what we are doing with our money right now and how we need to change in order to achieve our aspirations. I suppose in many ways it is the first step in divorcing yourself emotionally from the business.

It is business now, and you need to put your finances on a professional footing. As with other sections of this book, you are probably doing some things correctly right now but won't be doing others. Changes will need to be made, but as with most things, a gently, gently approach with gradual change will be a more practical way. So let's start by identifying some of the essential elements in your money management, and we'll look first at bookkeeping.

BOOKKEEPING

Keeping your books right as you grow is basic nowadays. This is a good time to assess where you are, who's doing the bookkeeping at the moment, what sort of a job they are doing, and more importantly how you should be doing it as you grow your business.

Now if you are already farming it out, or indeed have someone else dedicated to it in-house, that's great. You will have already realised what a time-stealer it is, and that maybe it is not one of your core competencies. In other words, you are better off managing the more positive aspects of the business, whether that is selling or product development etc. If you have already farmed it out, this is a good time to reassess what is being done now and whether you want to change it. In a normal bookkeeping set-up, your bookkeeper will probably actually physically write up the books, do your payroll (by that I mean keep the PAYE records for each of your employees and make the monthly returns) and will probably be doing your VAT returns and bank reconciliation. As well as that, they are likely to be working out whom you need to pay, drawing up your cheques for signature, and probably also advising you about who has not been paying you and what you need to do about that.

Is your bookkeeper actually doing all this for you? Could they be doing some of these things if they are not doing them already? Are you now reaching a stage where you should be looking at bringing this bookkeeping in-house by taking on a full-time employee?

If you have not reached the stage yet where you have farmed your bookkeeping out, you must realise that it involves a huge time commitment, often being done late at night when you are physically exhausted and not at your mental peak. It is time to make the move.

Good bookkeepers could come into your business on a part-time basis initially. That is probably preferable to their taking away your books to their own offices. The reason for that is that they will have a better understanding of how your business operates if they are working on site, and they will be beside you to deal with any queries as they arise.

You may be considering whether you need a full-time or a part-time service, or whether you should be looking at this stage at building up your finance department by employing an accountant yourself. If you are serious about growing the business, at some stage that is going to have to become a reality and you are going to have to bite the bullet in terms of its cost.

KNOWING YOUR KEY PERFORMANCE INDICATORS (KPIS)

In most businesses there are two or three key areas which, if you keep an eye on them properly and act on if they get out of kilter, will ensure the financial health of the business as you grow. Knowing these two or three key performance indicators (KPIs), will mean you have a good knowledge of the foundation blocks of your business. This means that if you keep these figures at the front of your mind, and these figures only, you will have your finger on the pulse while you spread yourself out over all the other areas of the business.

For many businesses these KPIs are based around sales growth, gross profit margin and wage costs, although they may be different in your own business. It is likely that intuitively you have a good feel for these indicators, but if you are not doing so already, it is now time to formalise them into an actual number.

For example, in our business a really important KPI is wage costs as a percentage of sales. It's something we monitor every week in every store—and it's hugely important to our bottom-line profitability. As the weekly ebb and flow of the business shows, the figure can vary substantially from one week to the next, especially in a small business.

Let's say our target wage cost is 25 per cent of net sales. Over the course of a number of weeks, we monitor and discover that, on average, our wage costs are running at 29 per cent of net sales. This extra four per cent is straight off our bottom line. It's fixable by paying attention to it and making adjustments to how you are staffing the business. It could also be a sign that retail prices need to increase because wage rises, rather than staffing levels, are eating into profitability.

The point is that if you have an idea of what is going on, you have some chance of dealing with it—but if you don't . . .

UNDERSTANDING CASH FLOW
Cash is often referred to as the life-blood of business. Understanding the difference between cash and profit is basic. Realising that no matter how good your business is, if you run out of cash you're bust, can be harder to understand. This is particularly difficult if you have a business where sales are growing strongly but you can't finance the production.

SECURING YOUR CASH
It is not easy to make sure that the cash your customer pays you actually reaches your bank account. I can't think of any business owner I know, particularly in retail, who has not suffered from cash being ripped off by a member of staff. Notwithstanding your need to trust people if you want to grow, cash is a huge temptation to a lot of people—and if you make it easy for them, and particularly if they get away with it once, they will take advantage of your weakness.

It follows that you need to have systems and processes in place which at least make your staff think you know much more about what's going on than you do. Taking your cash really seriously will also filter down to your staff. For example, here are some things you could do:

- Treat cash shortages and overs really seriously (overs can mask a fraud as much as an under)

- Don't take stock yourself without paying for it fully
- Make thieving a dismissible offence—no second chances for anyone
- Analyse your cash daily
- Make one person responsible for its management
- Install cameras if appropriate

DEBT COLLECTION

Collecting your money is a good example of why you need to divorce yourself emotionally from the money side of the business. I know in my early days I had 'friends' who owed me money and who I knew were experiencing financial difficulties of their own. I didn't feel able to chase them too hard for the money they owed me. This is no way to grow your business. This seat-of-the-pants approach won't work for ever—you will lose some contact because of the sheer number of customers you have as the business grows, and the fact that you will not know them and their particular businesses as well as you did in the early days.

Debt collection is a catch-all phrase for looking at your credit terms. For example, how many days are you theoretically actually *giving* versus how many days your creditors are actually *taking*? You should be looking at basic business clauses, like retention of title, meaning that you retain ownership of the goods you have sold until the debt is paid. You might also look at why you would extend more credit to somebody who already owes you a fortune. Do you need to cull your customer base to take out the ones who are not worth the hassle? How are you chasing your bad debts? Do you use a 'repo man'? At what stage do you write off a bad debt or go legal?

Getting strict about your credit control sends a signal to the people you are doing business with that you are taking it seriously. You will earn more respect from your peers by being tough but fair, than by being sloppy and letting things slide. It is human nature for people to take advantage of a sloppy money-collection department.

The other thing you could look at is, could you justify employing a credit controller either on a part-time or full-time basis?

PRODUCTION OF MANAGEMENT ACCOUNTS

Producing monthly management accounts is pretty basic. In fact you could say it is a real key performance indicator (KPI) to make sure you have them by the twentieth of the month following the month that has just passed.

Now the thing with management accounts to my mind is they do not have to be absolutely accurate—that is what the audit is for—but they are there to spot 'trends', particularly in your KPIs.

Management accounts are one of the real engines of a business, providing motivation when you are doing well, and absolute clarity when you are not. We use them to measure actual performance against plans. The only certainty with plans, of course, is that they will be wrong. What the management accounts will help you sort out is the scale of your 'wrongness'. You will either be doing better than you think or worse than you think, but you certainly won't be doing what you *thought* you would be doing.

You should use management accounts not only to see where you are straying from your plan, but also how you are doing against the long-term plan for the business. They help keep you focused when events of the day conspire to drive you down a particular path that may have no bearing on what your ultimate plans are. When you start doing management accounts, they usually consist at first of a profit and loss account, balance sheet and cash flow together with revised projections (revised to take into account what is *actually* happening).

As the quality of your financial information improves and you get used to having them on time, you can expand them by including the KPIs of the business and tracking problem areas that need attention, which you will then remember to look at for the next set of accounts.

If you are not doing them already, you need to start. This is key, if you are serious about growing. If you are already doing them, maybe it is time to have a look at the way you are doing them, and the quality and type of information you have in them. Our management accounts have really evolved into a management report, the main part of which is the management accounts but which also includes reports on other areas of the business as well. This might be a good idea for you to think about at this time.

MANAGEMENT MEETINGS

It would be hard to believe that you were serious about growing your business right now if you are not running regular meetings of one sort or another. You are probably already running management meetings. I know my colleagues used to hate them as I'd let fly at our regular get-togethers. I have moderated a bit since then, but when we are all so busy travelling or buried in niche areas of the business, meetings are so easy to overlook or let slide.

Regular communication is the bread and butter of a growing business. We need to meet and communicate with each other and, like it or not, the money is the engine for everything else, so it should be the core around which the rest of the meeting revolves.

It is actually a real discipline to make sure that meetings do happen when they are supposed to happen. For example, a sales meeting is essentially about increasing sales or money through the business.

You may already be having other meetings internally, for example, weekly sales meetings or weekly mini catch-ups on a Monday morning—they are all good. But your management meeting every month should be the big one—the one everyone knows they have to attend, for which they have to be well prepared, and in which they are going to be held accountable.

Usually we review the management accounts, comparing actual to budget. We then review the business under the main headings of sales, production, people etc. and make action points for the next meeting. One idea we have adopted is to have key management people in the business, who are not necessarily directors or usually at senior management meetings, attend and present on their part of the business to senior management. This 'bloods' them and gives senior management a chance to see the talent which they might otherwise not see.

As with all meetings, people should be prepared before they get there and the chairman—in other words you—should, before the meeting starts, outline the agenda, the objectives for the meeting and at what time the meeting will finish.

BUSINESS UNITS/PROFIT CENTRES

As your business grows you should start to get an understanding of each of the component parts of the business, and the effect each has on the whole. In other words, you need to start to micromanage the business. You are trying to find out what areas are making the money for you, as opposed to those you assumed were.

We have reached the stage where we almost have a separate business plan for each different business area. And as you grow you may well have managers in charge of each one. In O'Briens we reckon we run two essentially separate businesses. One is the business of selling and developing our franchises, where we have a relatively small number of customers who come in and spend hundreds of thousands of euro on a new franchised store. The second one is the retail business, where we have thousands of customers coming in spending relatively small amounts of money and repeat-purchasing frequently. In our franchising business we break our profit centres down into geographic areas by country. But in the retail business we do it not only by country but also by category, for example, food, hot beverages, cold beverages, snacks etc.

By having a proper understanding of the key components of the business, we are able to bring on the areas that are proving profitable for us, look at dropping the areas that are not, and alter the whole mix of products so that ultimately we achieve our financial objectives.

STAFFING THE FINANCE AREA

As you look at most successful businesses that are growing to the medium-size stage, you will notice something they all have in common. They nearly all have a business led by a CEO and a finance director. You will notice it is not a CEO and a marketing or sales director, or a CEO and a production director. It is a CEO and a finance director. And the reasons for this should be blatantly obvious by now.

It is unlikely for most of us, as we grow from small to tall, that we would be ready to take on a finance director immediately. But it is something to keep at the back of your mind as you start to hire people into your finance department. In a purely business sense this position is the next most important management position after your own. Many companies wait until they get to a position where they can afford a finance director, but it is also usual to start by taking on an accountant or someone in the bookkeeping role who will eventually grow into that position.

THE IMPORTANCE OF GETTING A GOOD ACCOUNTANT

Getting a good accountant for my business was one of the best business decisions I made. If you look at your current accountants, would they inspire you not just with the quality of their accounting advice but also as your close business advisers? Do they have your best interests at heart? Are they bringing something to the party over and above their technical skills?

If there is a question mark over them, then you should take steps to meet other accountants until you find one you're completely comfortable with.

Brody's 3 ideas for managing your money

- Mind your cash—literally and figuratively
- Figure out three financial KPIs for your business
- Get an accountant you're totally comfortable with

Chapter 9
Scaling Up your Output

Scaling up involves all of the different areas of the business. In this section we're looking at producing your output—whatever that is—on a bigger scale, better and more efficiently. The ideas in this chapter are designed to stimulate your thinking, as there may be many other areas which are relevant to your own business but not covered here.

Let's start by looking at something I think is one of the very cornerstones of a successful business—the idea of being really good at one thing. My proposition is that if you can find out what it is in your business that theoretically you can be excellent at, or the best in your market at, then it is something that will be infinitely scalable.

THE IDEA OF BEING GOOD AT ONE THING

If someone asked you today what is the one thing that your company is best at, the one thing your company really stands out for, or the one thing you are most proud of, would you be able to answer them? Picking out one thing that your company can do better than anyone else seems to me the essence of most successful growth businesses. And while it is probably true to say it is very difficult to become the very best in the world at something, the process of trying to achieve that goal is both healthy and good for your business for lots of reasons.

Think of a company like Coca-Cola—around for more than 100 years making brown, sugary water—and that is pretty much it! Coke still spend untold millions of dollars every year on research and development into their product, and you would think that all there was to be known about selling brown, sugary water had already been discovered. Yet they're still trying to find out how to do it better. They also spend countless millions of dollars every year advertising their brand. Now you would think that everybody in the world must know about Coca-Cola at this stage, and yet they feel the need to constantly reinforce the strength of their brand by advertising the fact. As the undisputed leaders in the world at selling brown, sugary water, one curious fact you will notice about Coca-Cola is that they tend to concentrate on that, and not to try and sell too many other things.

Take the Levis brand—also around for 100 years or so. Levis have become a household name by selling blue denim jeans. Now you would think that all there is to know about making blue denim jeans had already been discovered, yet Levis continue to spend millions of dollars every year figuring out how to make blue denim jeans even better than they have been making them for the last 100 years. On top of that, they spend millions of dollars annually advertising their brand. You would imagine that anybody in the business of buying blue jeans must know about the Levis brand, yet they continue in a relentless fashion to make sure that their brand name is at the forefront of people's minds when they are out buying clothes.

You will notice an interesting thing about Levis: they do not attempt to make brown, sugary water or any other products. They are not stupid in Levis, no more than they are in Coca-Cola. They do it for a reason, and that is to stay on top of their market category.

A much more recent example is my current favourite, the British brand Innocent Drinks. Innocent is another example of a company very narrowly focused on being the best in the world at pre-packaged smoothies. While they do not have the budget of Coca-Cola or Levis, they still spend considerable amounts of their turnover on research and development and on marketing, to figure out how to make and market smoothies even better than they currently do.

The logic of this is inescapable. The world is full of mediocre businesses, businesses that are to some extent good at lots of things. In fact, I would say the vast majority of firms are mediocre, and that is why they never become truly great companies. Think of your average downtown diner restaurant. They will sell you a sandwich, pasta, pizza, chicken and chips, possibly quiche lorraine, lasagne and salads as well. Do you notice how most restaurants like that do not seem to grow or expand? Could it be because they are kind of good at each of the products they do, but aren't really excellent at anything? Because they don't specialise, they don't reap the benefits of knowing their market intimately. They don't have customers singing their praises and they can't achieve the profits of a specialist chain because essentially it is an inefficient business.

When we set up O'Briens as a business, I understood this simple concept and so we set out to be the best in the world at selling sandwiches and coffee. We also wanted to be the best franchise company in the world. If you visit one of our stores it will be perfectly obvious to you that we are not the best in the world at selling sandwiches and coffee. Notwithstanding 20 years of effort, we still don't get it right all the time and we are constantly striving to do it better and to improve. Like us in O'Briens, by picking one area where you really want to be the best, you become very narrowly focused on that one thing, you will learn all about it and in the process become expert on it, and that will give you a competitive advantage. That is why companies like Microsoft, Anglo Irish Bank, Ryanair and Airbus became so successful. It is from essentially focusing on one product: Microsoft on user-friendly software, Anglo Irish Bank on property-based commercial lending, Ryanair on low-cost

short-haul flights and Airbus on manufacturing large commercial airliners.

But what if you are in a business where you have to offer a lot
of services, like a hotel? I remember one hotel owner arguing
with me. He said, 'We have to have great rooms, a superb
restaurant, a really good spa and a golf course to boot. If we take
your line of reasoning, we can't do it because we can't possibly be
the best in the world at all of these things.' And that's true; but it is
possible to pick out one of the services you offer as the one that
defines you: 'Yes, we have a great hotel with our lovely rooms and
a beautiful spa, but the one thing that really sets us apart is our
fantastic golf course.' Or it could be 'We have a great hotel with
beautiful rooms, a beautiful spa and a golf course, but we are most
proud of our award-winning restaurant.' You get the idea. If we
sometimes just *copy* what the big guys are doing or those we aspire
to be like, it is not a great basis for building a business. But
copying their *methods*, particularly ones that most of them use
and are proven in action—now that's not a bad strategy.

Setting your sights on being a really great company by doing
one thing as well as you possibly can and then focusing
relentlessly on achieving that goal, will set you well on the road
towards growing from small to tall. Before we look at how to
scale up your output—when you have decided what it is you can
be best at—let us have a quick look at what we think is the
blueprint for the expansion of the business.

GETTING THE BLUEPRINT RIGHT—QUALITY, SERVICE AND PRICE

Three features of your organisation that are almost universal in
their difficulty to get right are quality, service and price. Get any
one, or worse, two of them wrong, and you're in big trouble.
Having said that, it's almost impossible to get them all rocking
simultaneously because, for example, low prices and great
service are basically incompatible.

Most companies concentrate on getting two of the three
right.

Ryanair concentrate on price and quality and forget about service, and that works for them. The Four Seasons Hotel group concentrate on quality and service and almost forget about price. The Northern Rock banking group, who grew to fame by having the first modern 'run' on a bank, grew large on price (the best interest rates on deposits) and quality (they were an internet bank). When one of the two features they majored in went wrong (quality—their website crashed and customers couldn't access their savings), they would have folded except for the intervention of the Bank of England. Think about your business. What two features would be logical for you to major in?

Pricing itself can be difficult to get right. It is one of those things a lot of us do by trial and error. Pricing should be determined by a formula and the reality of the market around you. We covered the way to do a simple break-even analysis in the Managing Your Money section. This will often show that your pricing isn't right and in fact that you need to increase it. I twigged early on that it is not a good idea to advertise your price increases. I remember at the very beginning, when we did have to raise our prices, putting a sign up in the shop to advertise that and to apologise to customers because we were doing so. I quickly realised that most people didn't notice the price increase, but by drawing attention to it we made it a much bigger issue than it needed to be.

Recently I got a call from a very concerned franchisee of ours who had just put the prices up for some of his product, and had an awful time with his customers. He said to me that the price increases were unsustainable and that he would be left with no option but to bring the prices back down again tomorrow, otherwise he would be out of business. I then asked him exactly how many people had actually complained about the price increases. He said only two had, but one of them had given him a really hard time and made a big fuss in the shop in front of a lot of customers. I then asked him how many people he had served that day, how many transactions he had through the till, and he said that it was a normal kind of day—he had done about 300 transactions. Two people out of 300 does not lead to an unsustainable price increase, and I said to him, 'Look, leave the prices up for a week. If you really feel you can't live with them after a week, let's look at them again, but I think you are only hearing the customer who complains the loudest, and he isn't all your customers.' Our franchisee did as I asked and I never heard from him again—and the prices didn't come back down.

SHOULD YOU CONSIDER OUTSOURCING?

Outsourcing is one item you should consider as you look at whether your blueprint is as good as it could be right now.

For a lot of businesses in manufacturing, it became inevitable over the last few years as production costs were simply much lower abroad. What happened for manufacturing also happened for some service sector industries like data processing and call centres.

It may be more than obvious that your business is not suitable for it, but is that really true? Could there be ancillary parts of your business, for example, handling tele-sales, that could be done better, at a cheaper cost, by getting a specialist to do them?

Part of the audit of your blueprint is to consider just that.

SYSTEMISING THE BUSINESS

So having ascertained the blueprint is as right as we can get it, we need to turn our attention to systemising the business— putting repetitive processes and systems into some kind of order. Where in the past you may have had the organisation of your business stored away in your memory, you now need to involve other people, and to systemise the process so that it can function effectively in your absence. Systems engineering as a science is how great companies get it right—from production to service to sales to profits. Management guru Tom Peters talks of systems being five per cent about technical processes and 95 per cent about the attitude of the people.

We discovered in O'Briens that you can have the best systems in the world, but if the franchisee or the manager isn't up to it, the best systems in the world won't compensate for that fact. Let me give you an example. Since we started our business, we have written down in a series of manuals the best way to do something. This was done as we figured it out, so that we could share that best practice among our franchisees. Over the years that has built up into a fairly impressive set of documents which lists in very fine detail how to run one of our O'Briens businesses. When a new franchisee starts with O'Briens, they all get much the same training, and they all get a set of these manuals with which to operate the business. You might expect new franchisees would get on much the same, but as we have found out, attitude is an important part of running the business. If the franchisee is coming in with, for example, preconceived notions that hygiene isn't terribly important, then they will tend to run a dirty shop. If somebody else comes in with the view that serving customers is demeaning to them or below them, then guess what—the customer service is not going to be great. If somebody comes in who is not disciplined and organised, then they are going to struggle to make any money out of the business because being disciplined and being organised is part and parcel of achieving margins. It just reinforces the importance of attitude as opposed to technical process. However, what we are looking at now is technical process.

MANUALISING THE BUSINESS

One of the ways you will be able to roll out on a bigger scale is by manualising your operations so that you don't have to reinvent the wheel every time you do a job. It is vital, of course, as we saw when we looked at the blueprint, that if you want to systemise something, it already works in one way or another. In our business as we developed it, we wrote down best practice for others to share, and we discovered almost by accident that it brought all sorts of rewards. For instance, we set standards which everyone in the organisation understood and shared. We set specifications, for example, for our Triple Decker sandwich. These said that a Triple Decker had to be made in a particular way: you started with the bread, got a layer of butter, it had its bacon added and its coleslaw, then the toast went on, then the lettuce, then the tomato and the onion, and then finally the top slice of bread. It was then cut on the diagonal and served in a particular way. You might think on the surface that systemising something as simple as making a sandwich is a bit like teaching your granny how to suck eggs, but everybody approaches the process with a different knowledge-set and a different idea of what it should be like. By writing it down and being explicit about how it is built and how it is served, we have eliminated the guesswork.

- Manualising the business made it easier to train people. We now had a simple document which explained in black and white how to do the task; we could train people how to do it; and then they could take away the manual as a reference for whenever they needed it.
- Manualising the business ensured consistency—we're all singing from the same hymn sheet; we're all building our Triple Deckers in the same way; we're all operating our shops in more or less the same way.
- It helped us to make people accountable. For example, if you train somebody in how to do a job and give them manuals to back it up, there really is no excuse for not doing the job properly. We found that before we manualised the business, people would blame their lack of understanding for some-thing not happening, and sometimes that was partially true. But when we had the training and the manuals in place, we found that that excuse became more and more untenable.
- Finally, it helped us simplify the business, making it more efficient and more profitable as we went along.

Manualising the output of your business means breaking the production process down into mini-jobs. For example, to open a new O'Briens store we broke the process down into a series of mini-jobs and we put those mini-jobs into a series of manuals.

We now have a Shop-fitting Manual which explains, in minute detail, how to construct an O'Briens store. We have a Store Opening manual which is essentially a 90-day countdown before the store opens, listing what needs to happen on a particular day so that we arrive at the opening day and everything is in place. We have a Staff Manual which we use to train and induct new staff into the business, and of course the backbone of our business is our Operations Manual, which details how to manage the business, how to deal with the people involved, how to merchandise, how to market the business, how to look after your money and where to buy supplies.

The process of opening a new business seems simple on the surface. However, it is actually crowded with thousands of tiny details, all or the majority of which need to be in place in order for the store to open effectively and profitably. All the stakeholders involved in opening the new business—from ourselves as the franchisor, to our own support staff, to the franchisee, to the architects, the shop fitters, the equipment suppliers, the food suppliers, to the new staff—all are working from the same set of books, from the same template, and this ensures that 95 per cent of the time we get it right. Funnily enough, the five per cent of the time that we don't get it right, it is the people bit, the management bit, that isn't being done effectively—not the manuals bit.

Manualising your business helps to make sure you get things done the way you want them to be done, that you get them done consistently, and that you are able to impart the knowledge you have to other people.

Part of the process of breaking the tasks down in your business into many jobs is also to split the business up, in other words, to departmentalise it. This means the various aspects of running your business become specialist tasks in their own right. A typical growing business might have some or all of the following departments:

- Purchasing
- New product development
- Human resources
- Sales and customer relations
- Production
- Accounts and finance
- Strategy

As your business grows, specialist management in these various areas of the business becomes the norm, and you step more and more out of the day-to-day nitty-gritty to being the leader.

SCALING UP BY ACQUISITION
Growing your business by buying another company can be an effective strategy for scaling up. Potential acquisition targets will usually come under one of these headings:

- A competitor of yours, whom you can eliminate while adding their sales and production to your companies
- A business in a new area or country you want to move into strategically
- A supplier that can reduce your input costs, while giving you greater control over the production process
- A publicly quoted company that you can reverse into and avail of their stock market listing to publicly trade your shares

The target company can usually be paid for with cash, new shares in your company, a deferred loan note (where you agree to pay all or some of the purchase price at some time or event in the future), or a mixture of the above.

Acquiring a business requires specialist advice, your accountant being your likely first port of call.

THE POTENTIAL DIFFICULTY OF INTEGRATING AN ACQUISITION
Finding a company to buy and agreeing a purchase price are often the easier aspects of acquiring a business. Integrating the

two businesses together can often be a fraught, expensive and time-consuming affair. Issues to consider include:

- The compatibility of your IT systems
- The hierarchy of management of the combined entities
- The different cultures of the two organisations

Brody's 3 ideas on scaling up

- Be good at one thing
- Price, quality and service—concentrate on getting two of the three right
- Manualise your repetitive processes

Chapter 10

Great Teams give Great Service

JOE'S STORY

Joe Carey is an employee on the Ulster Bank team. Aged 31, he is a customer adviser in a busy Dublin city-centre branch. Joe has worked for Ulster Bank since he left school as indeed his father did before him. Joe had secretly dreamt all his life of being a professional soccer player, but an injury to his knee in his teenage years put an end to that. He does his work, is quiet and is considered reliable by his workmates. He does enough to get by but certainly doesn't push himself. He is ambivalent in his attitude to the bank. His salary pays for his lifestyle and as long as he doesn't screw up too badly, he may keep the job until he retires.

He has done many training courses with the bank—on credit control, on time management, on finance for non-financial people; indeed, he has even done courses on customer service! For Joe these are an entertaining diversion from his mundane life. The truth is that Joe is bored by his job. He is bored being part of the Ulster Bank team. He knows he is not cut out for greatness—another 25 years of the same stretches ahead. He can't seem to do anything about it.

Joe, in fact, lives for football.

Where he is bored by work, Joe comes alive when mention is made of the beautiful game. When he's not working he is either watching, talking about or dreaming about football—his absolute passion in life.

Joe is a Shelbourne supporter and when Shels are playing at home, he never misses a match. Naturally he is a member of the Supporters' Club and as a member of that team he lives the experience of the players on the field. When they score, which they're doing frequently at present, he is clearly delighted. When they lose, he takes it personally. When a player disagrees with a referee's decision, Joe feels the same heady mix of frustration and anger as the player does.

On match days, particularly during the week, Joe rushes home from work, decks himself out in the latest Shels jersey, scarf and hat and heads for Tolka Park. On the way he stops into Fagan's in Drumcondra to meet up with his mates for a few pints before the match.

They're all dressed the same. When they get to the match and take their places in the stand, Joe becomes totally engrossed for the couple of hours he's there. He shouts and roars, screams and groans, is ecstatic and depressed, all in the space of 90 minutes. When he gets home, and particularly if Shels have won, he is sated and satisfied, feeling he has played his part in getting his team to victory.

WHY THE STORY?

It might seem like a funny story to tell at the start of a chapter about customer service, but if you believe as I do that good customer service comes from good teams—great customer service comes from great teams—then talking about teams and team leaders and team members seems like a good place to start.

Let's look at some ideas around the theme that great customer service comes from great teams. Let's also look at what you could change in your own businesses, the changes you can make with your own teams tomorrow that will put you well down the road to delivering great service.

I'll bet there are a fair number of people reading this book who think the customer experience is not really relevant to them. Because they don't deal with customers personally, they think this section is really for someone else. Wrong—as you will see. If you have even one person who reports to you, then this customer service notion is aimed specifically at you, and in fact not, as you might think, at the frontline staff.

I approach this issue as someone who has been trying to get customer service right in my own business for the last 18 years. And believe me, we're a long way from where we want to be. It's not something that just gets fixed and then you never look back. Trying to get it right—really believing that you can effect change—is the important thing to embed in a company's culture. Great customer service can't be embedded; treating it seriously and appropriately can.

In Joe's story, he is a member of two teams—his work team and his football team. Wouldn't you agree that his performance in both teams is wildly different?

If we could get Joe to perform in work to the same level of intensity as he does in his football team, do you think that would make a difference to his output? Do you think if Joe felt about work as he does about football, the effort he was prepared to put into giving great customer service would improve?

You know great customer service doesn't come from people who are taught to be parrots and to trot out the same old lines. It comes from those who are basically happy in their work. And that's what I want to go through in this section—the notion of fulfilled staff giving great service.

THE DIFFERENCE IN THE TEAMS

Let's go back for a minute to Joe and his teams. Let's try and understand why Joe has a completely different attitude to both. Let's start by looking at Joe as a person.

Joe has basic needs as a human. Some of his needs are met by his work and some are met by his pastime.

In his work Joe satisfies some of his needs, his need for **certainty**, for example:

> Joe likes to know that his salary will be there every month; he likes to know he will have a job to go to next month, and if he doesn't mess up he will have a job the month after that as well.

Obviously it satisfies his need for **money**; he has bills to pay and a lifestyle to finance.

What other needs does his work satisfy?

His football team, however, meets a completely different set of needs for Joe. Firstly there's his need for **uncertainty**. For as much as he likes certainty in his life, he also enjoys uncertainty—all humans do. In its extreme form, it's why people bungee jump or do whitewater rafting or race cars. Football is uncertainty with rules. He may get hurt emotionally, but he's unlikely to die from it. Not knowing the outcome before a game starts meets this need of Joe's.

Then there is his need for **significance**. Joe's an important member of the supporters' team—at least in his eyes he is. He is proud to wear the red and white of his team—Joe's team. His friends who are also supporters know he takes the whole business very seriously, and that makes him feel important.

Joe feels he makes an important contribution to his team. Without people like him to encourage the players, the other team might gain the upper hand. He puts time, money and effort into his team, and he gets no reward for it other than the pleasure of being part of their success, or indeed sharing the pain of defeat when things don't go so well.

He likes the **sense of belonging** that this gives him. He really does care about and looks out for other members of his team. They're a special group, the Shels supporters, particularly those die-hards like Joe who stuck with the team through the hard times—not like the prawn-sandwich brigade who fly over to the big Premiership matches in England, ignoring their own home-grown teams.

There is one final thing that turns Joe into a star performer for his football team, and that is **goals**—actual goals. Joe understands clearly that to be part of the winning team they need to score more goals than the opposition. In fact they need to score just one more goal than them. This 'winning goal' is the objective of every game, and clearly understood by all the players and fans.

In fact, *all* of us are on *many* teams. Obviously, there's your work team which is why you're here, but like our man Joe you may well be part of a sports team. What about your family team? Usually there are two of them—your immediate family and your extended one. Many of us are part of teams in our community, like parents' associations, political parties, or doing a bit for the church or the Tidy Towns committee. Then we have a circle of friends and acquaintances—another team.

Why is it then that with so many different teams in our life, our performance varies so greatly from one to the other? We certainly feel different intensities with each one. And we do, don't we? If we really want to stay members of a team, we have a different set of standards and behaviours to ones where we don't want to stay.

Do you understand how Joe might feel about his teams?

HOW CAN WE MAKE JOE A RAVING LUNATIC FOR HIS WORK TEAM?

What I mean is that if we have an understanding about what makes us passionately interested in giving our all for one of our teams, which may or may not be our work team, then we as leaders, as bosses, as employers, might be able to tailor our behaviour better—or, if you like, our management *style*—so that we create the kind of teams that turn people like Joe into raving lunatics, or at least ardent enthusiasts.

Because here's the rub. Great work teams don't just happen. They're a direct reflection of our leadership—your leadership. And that can be quite a difficult concept to take in because it

means that it's not someone else's fault if the service ain't great—
it's *yours*.

YOU'RE RESPONSIBLE

As the leader you set the whole tone for your section. Your team
will to a large extent look to you to set the standards. Your team
will look to you to walk the walk and not just talk the talk. Your
own attitude to customer service will directly influence that of
your subordinates.

People are not parrots. Therefore great customer service does
not come from teaching people to be parrots. Rather it comes
from people who are essentially happy in their work. If you want
to give great customer service, you have to look after the people
who work with you.

I firmly believe that people are not bad. In almost any business
you can think of, bad or poor customer service is not given by bad
people. Poor customer service is given by badly managed people.
The fault doesn't lie with the frontline staff, but rather with the
managers who are charged with looking after them. Great
customer service comes from great owner/managers giving great
leadership and creating a great environment for their workers.

WHAT IS GREAT CUSTOMER SERVICE ACTUALLY LIKE?

A visit to a Four Seasons hotel, or to Conor McCarthy, my
mechanic, referred to later in Chapter 12, shows this great
leadership in action.

I myself bank in Bank of Ireland in Talbot Street in Dublin.
The manager there is called Angie. I'm the same as a lot of
customers now in that I hardly ever call into my branch, so I
don't expect them to know me. Yet every time I go into the
branch, one of the more senior members in the branch always
greets me by name. I get a lovely, warm, gooey feeling about
Angie and her team.

I don't necessarily have the same warm and gooey feeling
about the Bank of Ireland brand, but whatever I do think of it is
substantially helped by Angie.

The whole tone in that branch is set by her. She sends me notes when something notable appears about O'Briens in the newspaper. She has obviously taught her staff to recognise me and, I can only presume, other customers of the bank as well. There's a good—a busy good—atmosphere there. There's a lot of smiling among her team.

And isn't that the whole point about customer service—to turn customers like me into enthusiasts for the service? And there's one other aspect to Angie's service which appeals to Brody the businessman: it's not subject to budgetary constraints. No excuses: what Angie does costs some time but not necessarily money.

Yes, the staff are good in Kelly's in Rosslare, and in Sheen Falls in Kenmare and in the Bank of Ireland in Talbot Street in Dublin, but it's the owners and managers who create the environment for the great service, and, frankly, without them it wouldn't happen. They set the standard and they walk the walk—and isn't it amazing how staff will respond to that?

I believe that only half the reason our staff get out of bed in the morning is for the money. Sure, we all need to eat and clothe ourselves and live somewhere, but once our basic needs are satisfied we become concerned about other things, and that's the other half of the reason people come to work—reasons like a person's sense of self-esteem.

SELF-ESTEEM
When people feel part of a team, they stay in a job and try hard to do well. They share in the vision of where the business is supposed to be going they have a common goal with their work-mates when they have a shoulder to lean on when things aren't going well, and a pat on the back when they do well; a sincere thank you for a job well done. That's why people stay in a job and try hard to do well—it's not just for the money.

TAKING PERSONAL RESPONSIBILITY
I'm in a unique position in my job. For years I have been helping people open their own businesses under the O'Briens brand.

With these people essentially opening the same business, under the same brand, in the same types of location, selling the same products at the same price—you might expect that they might get on pretty much the same.

But they don't—in fact they get on very differently.

I have seen many businesses over the years. On the one hand, you have poorly run O'Briens businesses where the owner or manager has said to me, 'You can't get good staff any more. The ones I have are useless. There's no such thing as loyalty. They will leave this job for €1 more an hour to go and work for the competitors. The work ethic is gone in Irish people. Why should I bother training them when they're just going to leave anyway?'

But the language is different from our more successful businesses when it comes to talking about their people: 'I have a great team. They're really trying hard. I couldn't do it without them. They're hungry to learn, so I train them as efficiently as I can, accepting that for most of them, they're not here for a career and they will eventually leave.'

Same name over the door, selling the same range of products, in the same type of retail outlet, with staff paid the same rate. Guess which delivers better service?

Guess which business makes more money?

Staff don't leave jobs for €1 more an hour—at least it's not the main reason they do. They leave because they're not treated with respect. Because the environment they're being asked to work in is chaotic, because they're not trained properly, they can't see a way forward.

The Small Firms Association carried out an exit survey recently of 7,000 people who were changing jobs, over the course of a year. I was frankly astonished at the results.

What would you say were the main reasons people changed jobs in Ireland?

Reasons for people to change jobs

1. were unhappy with their managers
2. felt contribution was not recognised
3. because of lack of advancement
4. because of salary

So let's go back now to look at some ideas for how we can make some simple changes in the way we treat our people, the way we lead our people, some ways that will deliver the better customer service we're all striving for.

LET'S BE HONEST

Let's just start this final part by being honest.

For example, I think I can have a meaningful relationship with about 20 people in my work and not many more than that. By that I mean that I can know about 20 people, who they are, what they aspire to be, what's important to them, that they have a family—in other words, that I can take a personal interest in them.

As I grew my business, I was conscious of that, and as I passed that 20 milestone, I added a Number 2 to my team, who started building his 20 and took the pressure off me.

After a while I realised that it's what all successful businesses do. And in fact it's what this company does to a lesser or greater extent. It's not only businesses that do it, but armies as well, and other large organisations that have to manage large groups of people. That's why there's a whole hierarchy in armies from ordinary privates, to corporals and sergeants, right up to generals. Each organisation is broken down into one person managing a relatively small group of people.

The second thing we need to be honest about is that we as managers are much more comfortable with facts and figures, with terms and conditions and agreements on work practices, than we are talking about our people and what makes them tick, or how we can turn them into enthusiasts for the business.

Our logical brains are comfortable with process and order, but uncomfortable with feelings and emotions. Yet giving great service is much more about feelings and emotions than about facts and figures and processes. We need to be honest with ourselves about that. Let's look honestly at what we can do.

LEAD BY EXAMPLE

The whole tone for the customer service in your business is set by how the manager operates. If you are respectful with people, it is likely your staff will mirror that behaviour. I remember hearing one of our managers talking about our customers by describing them as the Taliban. Language like that sends strong signals to your staff.

There's the famous story from the US about the CEO of a Fortune 500 company who announced 5,000 job losses, followed a day later by an announcement that he had been awarded a $1,000,000 salary increase and that the company had bought an executive jet. I wonder how his staff felt about him.

Holding a door open, thanking customers for their business, cleaning up litter if it's dropped around the front of the store, listening to customers' comments good and bad—all send powerful signals to staff. If, on the other hand, you're not bothered to get to know your customers, aren't respectful of them, treat them like they're someone else's problem—then you can't be surprised at the outcome.

ENQUIRE ABOUT PERSONAL ISSUES

Given the number of people you will be trying to keep a close relationship with, it pays to be interested in their life outside the business environment.

For many years in the early days, I had a young girl working with me called Mary Devine (not her real name). Mary was 16 and a drop-out from the education system when she first came to work with us, but very bright and hard-working. I have found through the years that I can become very fond of some of our staff, and Mary was one of those. I delighted in the fact that she broke all the stereotypes of a girl from her background. She came from a part of Dublin which at the time had 40 per cent unemployment.

It wasn't the green fields and private schools of south County Dublin where she was reared. Her father was unemployed, the family was poor. Despite that, she was driven to get on, and did so, while becoming very loyal to me personally. She was one of the few people I really trusted.

Mary rapidly became a supervisor, and then when she was only 17, a store manager in one of our busy downtown stores, where she managed a mixed crew of staff, for the most part very well. Unfortunately Mary had a ne'er-do-well boyfriend, and I was saddened to see a promising career falter when, still aged only 17, she came to tell me she was pregnant. She worked on for as long as she could, and shortly thereafter gave birth to her son James. Though she was happy to be a mother, her relationship with her boyfriend wasn't going well, and he was occasionally violent with her. She was also living at home and didn't get on too well with her father. Little James turned out to be hyper-active, so she was finding it really difficult to cope.

When James was about six months old, she moved out of her home and in with her boyfriend. As soon as she could arrange for her mother to help out with minding the baby, she came back to work part-time. Mary, I knew, found sanity and order in work where there was none in her private life, and in that sense work was her escape from her own reality and the mess she was in.

One morning I received a call from one of our staff to say that there was no one to let them into work. Because some of the stores had been opening consistently late recently, and we had had a staff meeting about it, I was livid. It happened to be Mary's store, and unfortunately I was beyond reason. I went down to open the store myself, and when Mary turned up at 10 am, two and a half hours late and without a phone call to explain herself, I let her have it. I was in no mood for excuses.

She burst into tears. It turned out that her boyfriend had beaten her up the night before. After midnight she had had to leave her flat with the baby and try and get into a women's refuge. The first one she tried was full, so they sent her—in her nightclothes—in a taxi to a second one, where they took her in. She had been so upset that they gave her a sedative to calm her down, and she had overslept. When she had awoken, she had had to go back to her flat to get some clothes and the baby's things.

I felt awful. Here I was reading her the riot act when she had just been through a most terrible experience. It taught me that you never know what's going on in people's private lives. I have taken it on board as one of life's lessons.

Communicate the vision

It's an old adage in business that it's very hard to get somewhere if you don't know where you're supposed to be going. To the extent that it's appropriate to communicate with your staff (obviously there's no point in sharing all your worries and concerns with them), it's always worthwhile to let your colleagues in on your plan, and to get them to buy into their part of it.

So we sit down with all our staff at the start of the year and talk about the year ahead. We get feedback from those working with us (which often produces a better plan). We also get an understanding of the bigger picture, and how the different parts of the business and the different people will interact.

Top teams know what they're about; they have a sense of purpose, and clearly measurable outcomes which they can get their heads around.

I have a wonderful team in O'Briens. There are about 30 of us in Dublin running a business in 12 countries. People who come into contact with our organisation for the first time comment on our people, that they're fired up about making a difference. I would confidently predict that if you asked any of our team what our objectives were as a business, they could tell you— because I tell them again and again and again.

Think about your team—what sense do they have of your goals? Do they buy into them; do they understand the part they have to play in them?

Regular thank yous

You can never say thank you often enough. It should be obvious to everyone that we respond well to a pat on the back, and we work harder and become more loyal as a result of frequent and sincere praise. If you keep a note of your associates, and remember to periodically single them all out individually to say thanks for a job well done, you will do more for customer service in the organisation than by almost any other act.

Have a sense of fun

There's no rule that says business has to be boring. While there's no doubt that there are lots of boring aspects to some jobs, you as the owner/driver have the power to use humour to create a great atmosphere in your workplace. Fun tends to be infectious so that your staff not only have a smile on their faces, but your customers do as well.

Southwest Airlines on the west coast of the US built a reputation for their wacky staff who lost no opportunity to ham it up in front of their customers. Restaurant chain TGI Fridays allows staff to choose their own head coverings, which gives staff a sense of individuality while providing a fun talking point with customers. Julian Richer, the founder of Richer Sounds, had a Rolls Royce available for staff who excelled in their work. The staff member was able to take the Rolls home to take their friends or parents for a spin.

Any of us can create a great atmosphere at work by having a laugh with our staff and customers. It doesn't cost money to create a good atmosphere—even in a bank!

Set the standard and continuously strive to reach it

Many of our businesses will be defined firstly by our staff and then by our standards. It goes without saying that we should all be striving to improve all of our standards all of the time. Having high standards is as much a personal approach to life as a business objective.

In truth, people have different ideas of what high standards are—many are prepared to accept standards that others find unacceptable. As you go through these exercises with your staff, you will find there are some who will not react to the new situation, no matter how hard you try. These people should in all honesty be moved away from the frontline—to be brutally honest, out of the business altogether, because they will unconsciously want to drag everyone down to their level of performance. The right people will have high personal standards which they will then encourage and coach their staff to achieve.

I suppose I am a perfectionist. I am never happy about the standards we achieve, which can make it very difficult for the people who work around me. I think entrepreneurs are generally perfectionists and the successful ones manage to pass this on to their staff. Being restless and unhappy about the standards reached means you are not complacent and are always trying to do it better.

Induct properly—train technically

It goes without saying that trained staff are a given in a service business like yours. Training is about systems and process and there should be no excuses in that regard.

During the height of Ireland's economic boom in the late 1990s, when there was essentially full employment, we had a kind of running joke about the difficulty of finding employees.

A new recruit would be interviewed at 9 am and then asked to start at 10. At 12 noon the new recruit was made a supervisor, and at 2 pm was appointed store manager. At 5 pm the new recruit was gone, never to be seen again. While the joke is deliberately exaggerated to make a point, it's maybe a bit close to the bone for some of us.

Imagine what a new recruit would think of his employer if he were not given the time to figure out how the business works before being asked to deal with customers.

Imagine what your customer feels like being served by someone who, through no fault of their own, hasn't a clue how to look after them. In O'Briens, perhaps unlike your business, we have the capacity to kill people if our training isn't up to scratch. Of all the things that keep me awake at night now, the prospect of a good food poisoning incident in a business like ours is the ultimate nightmare.

Giving the time to induct somebody properly into the new business more than pays for itself in the money you save by not having to continually advertise, interview and train a whole series of workers who start and then don't stick the pace.

Praise in front of others; admonish in private

None of us likes a bollocking. Nobody likes it being done in front of other people. If it's necessary, and it often is, to straighten someone out about their performance or their attitude, you will earn far more respect from your employee by doing it in private.

On the other hand, if you have something positive to say, you should shout it from the rafters. It's as important to catch your staff doing something right as it is to have negative conversations with them.

I was walking through one of our stores when a customer I knew beckoned me over. Retailing is one of those businesses where everybody else is expert at telling you how to run it, so I was fully expecting a lecture on one of the many shortcomings we have as a business.

Instead, she wanted to tell me about the really brilliant service she had received from one of our staff—Ann McLoughlin. Our customer had come into the busy store, struggling with a buggy and shopping. Ann had spotted her and asked some other customers to move to an adjacent table so our happy customer could sit down without blocking up the aisle. Ann had then taken her order and brought it down to her table (O'Briens is mostly a self-service business). I was delighted with the news and I decided to use it to my advantage.

'Ann McLoughlin, get over here this minute,' I roared in front of all the rest of the staff and indeed a shop full of customers. Ann was mortified. She feared the worst as she tried to make her way over to where I was standing. I put on my 'you're in big trouble' face as she approached. When she was standing beside me I said, 'Ann McLoughlin, this lady beside me called me over to say she's just had the best experience ever in O'Briens, because your customer service was exceptional. I know a lot of other people in this restaurant who work with you or who are served by you think you're fantastic too, so as your boss I just wanted to say thank you.'

Some people started to clap; our happy customer was beaming. Ann didn't know where to look; there were tears welling up in her eyes. It was a lovely moment for all the people in the store; everybody felt a little better going back to work or going home that evening because they shared Ann's delight. (Some time later she told me she had never been acknowledged like that before, by anyone, ever.) Shout your praise from the rooftops.

One common theme which you may have noticed in this chapter is that all these ideas for improving the customer service in your business don't have to cost money. In fact, most of them cost nothing at all to implement.

I might have used this chapter to write about fancy-pants techniques for retaining customers, up-selling, dealing with complaints—and there are good techniques out there—but in my experience, if the people bit isn't right, it's all just a waste of time and money.

Finally, before we finish up, let's look at our Joe again.

Joe isn't a bad person. He's not stupid. He's not lazy by nature. He doesn't mean to give bad customer service.

There are lots of Joes working in our businesses, lots of good people whom we're not reaching out to, people whose needs we're not meeting. And because we're not meeting them, they're going off to put all that positive energy and effort into other teams and pursuits. The challenge for us as managers is to stimulate them, to make them feel like champions, so that they can champion you and your business.

Brody's 3 ideas on team-building

- Having a good team starts and finishes with you
- People aren't bad—people who behave badly are usually badly treated
- Thank your staff as often as you eat

Chapter 11
Letting Go—Bringing on your People

WHERE AM I NOW?

As we think about growing our business from a small to a tall one, it is useful to think about where we are now, particularly in terms of how we're managing the business. For many of us, it could be: where I am now is that I like running my business; I am involved in all the decisions; I am really a happy autocrat. I am managing director, but also the financial director and the sales director. I am the accountant; I look after all the personnel. I am basically indispensable, but if I am truthful, I am also not doing all the things I should be doing. I am enjoying life; we are good at what we do, but I know there are lots more places to go and lots more places to bring this organisation.

WHERE DO I NEED TO BE FROM A MANAGEMENT PERSPECTIVE?

It's a simple idea, but we cannot keep on growing by doing the same things in the same way. It's also not possible to be all things to all people. The fact is that a lot of the jobs you are doing right now need to become specialised. Maybe not all today, but you need to think about starting the process.

For example, if you are doing your own bookwork at the moment, throwing out the work to an accounting firm is the first step on the road to employing your own accountant, and freeing up your time.

You need to make time for the important areas of the business, not just the jobs you have ended up doing because no one else wanted to, or the jobs you like doing the most.

Making time for the important stuff

You want and need to have time to grow the business. For example, you will need to figure out the KPIs, in other words, the key drivers of the business and whether that is margin or sales growth. You need to be able to keep on top of them.

You may need to front up the business for PR purposes. You'll need to motivate and build up the management and staff, interview new management and really try to bring on people better than yourself. These are some keys to how you are going to make the business grow. There will be others for your specific business and of course you'll need to have time to crisis-manage because life has a way of screwing up the best-laid plans.

Finally, you'll want to enjoy it and try to keep a balance between your working life and that outside.

How do I get there?

Well, having decided that you cannot continue to do things in the same way if you want to get a different result, you have to decide what it is absolutely vital that you continue to do, and what you can get someone else to do.

In other words, what are you so good at that is absolutely vital for the success of the business that you continue to do it?

Staying in control

Staying in control could be defined as:

- Knowing what's going on
- Making sure that what you want to happen does happen

By all means step back from day-to-day repetitive tasks that someone else can do, but not so far back that you lose touch with what's going on.

Bringing on a strong Number 2

You should always be looking to bring on a strong Number 2 in the business—someone who can back you up and act in your place when you're not around. Obviously, your Number 2 should be the best person for the job—not necessarily the person to whom you owe the most, or the person who has been the most loyal—and that can involve making difficult choices.

Number 2s often emerge from within the ranks of your employees, and that may be the best person you could possibly get; but if not, you should be prepared to go outside to get someone just right.

Get rid of the jobs someone else can do

The more important question to ask is: what is it that you have ended up doing because nobody else is doing it or because nobody else likes doing it, but really it is a complete waste of your time to be doing it?

Redefine what it is important that you continue to do

I could give you examples of some things that may be important for you to keep on doing, but they are only examples because they will be different from business to business. They could include the creative side, product development. For example, if you are the one in the business who comes up with new ideas for product development or improving the service, it may be important that you keep doing it.

Do the important hiring yourself

Hiring is a creative process and is the key to building a larger business. The quality of your business is a direct reflection of your people. Some things to consider as you expand your team:

- Sometimes it is worth making a job fit an exceptional person
- Timing of when to hire—when you can afford the negative cash flow
- Do the really important hiring yourself, but perhaps someone else is better at doing the others
- When you interview, look for buy-in, ability, hunger and a desire to be a team player

Hiring can be a very hit-and-miss process. A CV and an interview tell only part of the story. It's only natural that with a CV and an interview, a potential employee is in a selling mode, the same way we as employers are if we want someone to come and work with us.

There is nothing as good as getting a prospective employee in for a few days' orientation before you both make your minds up. That won't be possible for every position, but it can be the most effective method of making sure the new person is right.

Staying on top of your KPIS
Basic measures of how your business is performing, like the sales growth, new customer acquisitions, the gross profit margin, your wage costs as a percentage of sales and your development pipeline are probably key in any business. If you have a good understanding of them, it will help keep you on top of your game.

I can't know what they would be for your business, but there are certainly two or three KPIS that you just have to keep an eye on or else it can all start to get out of control.

Jobs you probably can't delegate
Making sure the brand standards are maintained and that **you remain as the brand guardian** or the rock of the brand is a really important job which can't be delegated. By that I mean that you are the final arbiter of what is acceptable, or how the products are developed, in the sense that they fit it with your view of the brand.

Let me give you an example of that: we developed O'Briens in the sandwich and coffee sector and, particularly in the early days, we had lots and lots of problems. When our retail sales through our stores were slow, there was a big temptation for us to go into wholesaling sandwiches or selling them to other retailers. One of our managers in particular thought it was a great idea in the sense of delivering top-line sales growth—and that was probably true. But I felt that it wasn't appropriate that other retailers should carry our brand, particularly if we were trying to franchise it and keep exclusivity in it, in the sense that you could only get an O'Briens sandwich in an O'Briens shop. But I also thought it was a distraction from our core business, which was retailing sandwiches and coffee. Wholesaling sandwiches is an entirely different business in my view, and that is not where I saw the future for the business. So I put a stop to it.

It may be important for you to **keep in contact with your key customers.** There are in most businesses a relatively small number of customers who account for the majority of the sales, and it is important that you make sure that they are happy to keep using you as a supplier. Clearly both you and key management need to maintain contact with those people, so that you know what they are doing—and they know what you are doing. You should then be able to nip problems in the bud before they become big issues.

Obviously a key role for you in your growth phase is **setting the strategy for the business** and then making sure the strategy is implemented, corrected as it goes off course, and stays focused on the original plan and vision.

THE JOBS I SHOULD BE GETTING RID OF FOR ME

What are the things that you shouldn't be doing? Well, I know in my business I ended up in the early days doing a lot of things that *other people did not like doing* or that other people thought were *boring*. Often I couldn't be bothered to train somebody to do them because it was *quicker to do them myself.* Similarly, I just ended up doing tasks, not for any particularly good reason, but that's just what *evolved*.

Here are examples of some of the things my survey of small business owners showed that the proprietors were doing that you may not need to be doing, and that somebody else definitely could be doing:

* collecting supplies from the supplier
* going to the wholesaler or the cash and carry
* doing lodgments
* dealing with every complaint: it is appropriate that as you bring staff on, they are empowered to deal with complaints themselves
* working on the shop floor: you should maintain a presence, but you do not need to be doing it all the time
* setting prices
* stocktaking
* being the receptionist
* delivering orders
* rostering

This isn't a definitive list. There are probably lots more things in your own particular situation which you know how to do best yourself, but equally there are lots of things that you are doing that somebody else could be doing as well or better. The knock-on effect is that delegating will free up the time for you to do what is important in terms of developing the business.

From doing this exercise you can now start to make decisions about what you can delegate and what is important for you to hang on to, as in the case of doing the books above, where you know you could pass the books to an accounting firm as a transition to getting in an accountant to work for you. The decisions don't have to be absolute; you know you have to be able to afford them, and that the process can be evolutionary rather than you doing it all at once.

The point is that while there are a number of things you should clearly keep doing, there are definitely others you should stop. This alone will free up much more of your time for productive purposes.

LEARNING TO TRUST—THE GREAT SECRET OF LETTING GO

You will have noticed that large, successful companies are invariably staffed by more than one person. From this you may have deduced that it's impossible to grow a big business on your own, and that you need people to help you. And if it follows that you need people, it also follows that you're going to need to trust them.

If you ask me for the single biggest reason why small companies stay small, I would say it's because the owners haven't learnt how to trust the people who work with them. Because of that, they are paralysed with fear that if they delegate certain 'important' jobs, their people will screw them up.

Yes, your people will do things differently to how you do them; yes, they will screw up as they learn new jobs; and, yes, they will make mistakes. But learning to trust is the only way you are going to be able to grow your business the way you want to.

One of the great things about trying people in new positions, with extra responsibilities, is that many of them will surprise you by doing them really well—God forbid they might actually do some jobs better than yourself! The risk, of course, is that sometimes your people will disappoint.

WE NEED TO WRITE IT DOWN AND MAKE A PLAN

So we now know what we need to do—to let go of at least some of our stuff—and we have decided what's important that we keep doing ourselves, and what somebody else can do. What do we do about it?

Well, having made a decision, you now need to make a plan, and as part of the plan you need to make a timeline. In other words:

- what you need to do overall
- what you are going to stop doing yourself and delegate to your people
- what you are going to continue to do, and indeed new tasks you will be taking on personally
- when you're going to do it by
- measurable targets for you and your staff so you can measure how you're doing

When you have made your plan, you then need to execute the plan and review it as you go along. As you review it, you need to make changes because it is certainly not going to work the way you thought it would at the beginning. And having made those changes, you then review it again and make further necessary changes.

Your main objective with this process as part of your small-to-tall growth is to make yourself dispensable. Let's look first at your priorities. You should prioritise the re-allocation of your jobs in terms of their importance to you as, for example, a time stealer.

Give a man a fish and you feed him for a day; teach a man to fish and you feed him for life

It is not fair to expect people to do new jobs and take on new roles and responsibilities if you have not trained them how to do those jobs or take on those roles. So part of this process is to identify where skills need to be upgraded and plan those upgrades or training accordingly. Now, as I have already said, some of your management and staff will amaze you in that they seem to discover this hidden talent when you put them in charge of something. These people will be key in your growth strategy and it will pay you to mind them and look after them well.

These people are the ones you want to keep, so you need to put in place incentive and bonus schemes if you do not already have them, and indeed consider a share option scheme if that is not already part of what you do.

But there's pain in growth

As you discover all these hidden talents among some of your staff, painfully you will discover that some of them will not be able to keep up with the new order. Many will not be able to grow with you or will not want to grow (or change) with you.

Despite your best endeavours, you may reach a stage with some of these people where you will either have to let them go or overlook them as promotion prospects come up. This is one of the most difficult and potentially destructive aspects of growing the business. Here are a small number of people working with you, many of them since the very beginning, who sweated, put themselves out for you, who are loyal and, in truth, whom you love and feel are part of your family.

I have had to make horrible decisions about people on a personal level. I try to divorce myself from my emotions and look at the business consequences of *not* taking action. On the one hand you have a friend who feels betrayed and rejected by your decision to let them go, and on the other hand you have a greater responsibility to the business and to the larger 'family' that will remain. But if they cannot and will not rise to the challenge with you, you have to be true to yourself. You can't maintain the status quo and grow the business at the same time.

Don't interfere—HANDS OFF

Initially, there is a great temptation to interfere, particularly as your staff struggle with change. I found myself getting exasperated by people in the organisation doing things differently to me, slower than me, making mistakes because they did not understand something properly, or just screwing up the job I delegated to them. It took a huge amount of discipline to hang back, to let them get on with it, to learn from their mistakes and to become better at their jobs.

Also, it's not fair to be second-guessing every decision that your employees make. Accepting that things are going to be done differently, at different speeds, sometimes with a different outcome, is part of your personal maturity in the growing business. Your objective of going from small to tall can only be achieved by getting yourself out of the day-to-day and bringing on your people. Small steps backwards, as your employees struggle with the new order, are contributing to the great leap forward as your business now has a real prospect of growth.

Brody's 3 ideas on handing over the business

- Decide what you must continue to do and what you can let go
- Do the really important interviews yourself
- Learn to trust more

Chapter 12
Building your Brand

Have you ever noticed the warm, fuzzy feelings you associate with a very modern brand like Innocent Drinks? They have managed to create, in the minds of consumers, this picture of a cheeky little brand taking on the Goliaths of the soft drinks business, being run by almost-hippies, selling food that's really good for you, in a light-hearted, fun way. This is while you are paying a price for their tiny bottles that you wouldn't have considered just a few years ago. Innocent are anything but almost-hippies. This is a brilliantly clever company that understands totally what a brand is and how to create and manage it.

Every business has one—a brand, that is. There is a myth about that only really big companies have brands, but that is not true; even the smallest companies have a brand, and that is why customers come and shop with them.

Let me give you an example: your local doctor, although you might not think it, has a brand. His brand might encompass the fact that he is local; customers like to shop locally. It might encompass the fact that he is trusted, in other words, that he is going to make you or your family better, and that he is reliable and that he is consistent.

Let me give you another example. Conor McCarthy runs a small car-mechanic business and has been looking after my car for the past ten years or so. Conor offers me a great service. When the car is due for service, he calls to me to collect it and gives me a replacement car. He then takes my car away, services it and delivers it back. Without asking, he will valet the car and put a big paper wrapper over the seat so that I don't get damp from the foam he has used to wash it. I probably pay a bit more for the service from Conor but, to be honest, what he does for me as a customer is not about price. I rave about Conor to my friends. Conor's brand values are built around great service and his utter reliability.

Let's look at one more example, but this time of a big brand and a big business: Euro Disney. Euro Disney's brand is built around the fact that it has a very well-known name built up over decades. But this brand is also about providing a quality family experience. Effectively, what it does is relieve parental guilt because, ever since both parents have been working outside the home, they have felt perpetually guilty about the amount of time they are spending away from their children. Euro Disney has very cleverly tapped into this fact by recognising that if parents bring their kids to Euro Disney, in the parents' eyes it relieves that parental guilt.

The other thing they have built into their brand, in a very clever way, is that a visit to Disney qualifies as a so-called 'quality family experience'. In Ireland it's an almost must-do for the middle classes—a rite of passage. If you haven't 'done Disney', somehow you're an inadequate parent!

By building these three traits into their brand—a great name, relieving parental guilt, and providing a quality family experience—they attracted at the last count over 13 million visitors to Euro Disney in one year. By way of comparison, that is over 50 per cent more than all the tourists who came to Ireland the same year.

Brands are mostly about emotion and reputation. Emotion because it is about feelings. For example, 'We always go to

McDonald's because the kids have a great time' or 'I always buy Christian Dior perfume because it makes me feel good about myself.'

Brands are also about reputation, and for reputation you could read 'trust'. So 'I always bank with NatWest because I know they will look after my money' or 'I always buy a Toyota because they never break down.'

Let's look at some characteristics of a brand promise.

THE BAD BRAND PROMISE

Two well-known brand promises are Ryanair's 'You may choose your own seat on board' advertisement, and Bank of Ireland's 'Bank of Ireland's dedicated relationship managers are here to see your business through its different life cycles, providing financial expertise and advice at each stage.'

Take Ryanair first: 'You may choose your own seat on board.' How many times have I heard that one? You have just arrived at the departure-gate rugby scrum. That is after you have walked two miles from where you checked in (in Dublin anyway), had a row with the girl at the check-in because you did not know you had to pay extra for your checked-in bags, and after your 30-minute queue through the security screens, where you've had the humiliation of having your personal belongings sorted through by a fellow wearing the kind of search gloves that are used to find things in your bottom.

You are now standing in the rugby scrum, knowing full well that Ryanair will not give you a seat number because it is quicker and cheaper not to do so, while some young hostess drones out the mantra, 'You may choose your own seat on board.' I don't know about you, but when I hear it I have an urge to get up and shake her and say, 'We know why you are doing it; we know why you are doing it.'

Bank of Ireland's promise is even worse. As you know, all major banks now have what are called Relationship Managers for their business clients. This sounds great for customers like me—after all, you will now have a dedicated manager who will build a strong personal relationship with you, get to know you and your business, and make decisions because they are not just looking at black-and-white sheets of A4. But I have learnt that they default on this promise. The problem is that Relationship Managers are appointed to a particular branch or customer for only a relatively short period of time.

Incredibly, as I've discovered, this is a deliberate ploy on the part of the bank to make sure that you do not actually form a relationship with the Relationship Manager! The words of the brand promise say one thing, but the meaning is completely different.

For 'Relationship building' read 'Don't build a relationship at any cost.' For 'We want to serve you, our customer' read 'We want our money back first and foremost—we couldn't really give a toss about the relationship.'

These are examples of brand promises that aren't kept—you get the message.

THE GOOD BRAND PROMISE

Ronseal's wood varnish brand promise is the one we all strive for, but few of us manage to deliver: 'It does exactly what it says on the tin.' It's amazing to me that this simple brand promise became so famous, because it must mean that, in consumers' eyes, very few companies live up to their promises.

Examples of really well-executed brand promises are rare. That's why Innocent Drinks have built such a great reputation into their brand in such a short period of time. 'Little Tasty Drinks' mightn't seem like much of a brand promise, but they have made the product and the way they brand it into an art form.

Under-promise and over-deliver

It's really the simplest of possible messages about branding, but it's another one on which we so often fail. We get enthusiastic and exuberant about the benefits of our brand that we forget about the practical realities of delivering it.

Many inexperienced or unethical practitioners make wild claims about the benefits of their products. The snake-oil salesmen of the 1880s in the American Midwest became legends for claiming ever-wilder benefits from consuming their products: 'Will grow back limbs—Will let you live to 200—Will restore a full head of hair in three months' were some of the brand promises made.

If you make a claim like 'the world's greatest sandwich', you'd better be able to back it up, otherwise consumers will treat it with the scepticism it deserves. Treating it in a tongue-in-cheek way like Carlsberg's 'Probably the best lager in the world' works though, as it gets its message across while respecting the intelligence of the consumer.

Defined by excellence in one thing

As described in Chapter 9 about scaling up, great brands usually have a reputation for doing one thing really well. In Coca-Cola's case it is brown, sugary water; in Toyota's case it is reliable cars; in O'Briens' case it is sandwiches and coffee.

Keeping focused and keeping the message simple are at the core of great branding. Customers understand and remember simple messages.

Location is consistent with its brand

Having your location consistent with your brand is the basic premise of a brand value. For Sandymount Pet Hospital, its location in a small community is a key part of its brand value. The customers will shop with it because it is local.

On the other hand, the DHL Worldwide delivery business is predicated on the fact that it has offices all over the world, and because of that, it can offer a reliable next-day delivery service for customers. If DHL were placed in a small village like Sandymount as its only location, clearly it wouldn't instil customers with confidence that it could deliver on its brand promise.

Lives its ideals

A brand should be consistent with the impression it creates in the customer's mind. Euro Disney's reputation as a safe, fun place for a family to holiday has to be backed up by staff that respond to that message and greet children appropriately, and by making sure that, for example, sex shops are not located on the campus, which would be completely at variance with its ideals.

Consistent

Part of the strength of a brand is that it is consistent, in the sense that the product or service it provides is consistent from one day to the next and from one location to the next as appropriate. For example, the McDonald's brand is built upon the fact that you can buy a hamburger, fries and a Coke in a location in America and it will be pretty much exactly the same as you would get on London or Moscow or Tokyo. Customers place huge value in consistency because they know what they like and they like the familiar—particularly when they're in a strange location. People would sooner go for something they know than something they don't.

Offers a perceived value

Brands offer value to customers. McDonald's, as we mentioned, offers hygienically prepared, tasty food at a cheap price. The Four Seasons Hotel group offers outstanding customer service in an opulent environment.

A recent example of a brand that got into trouble when its perceived value declined was the internet-based bank, Northern Rock. Northern Rock was a large UK bank that managed to offer easily accessible internet banking and because it didn't have the overheads of high-street premises, was able to offer good value to customers by giving higher interest rates on deposits. This business model worked because customers trusted that they were going to be able to get their money out and that their money was in a safe place. When the Northern Rock bank experienced a run, the first one in modern times, their internet system crashed and customers found that the very basis on which they had deposited money with them, i.e. that they could get their money out again, was betrayed. It was a weird sight to see hundreds of customers lined up outside the physical offices of Northern Rock to withdraw their money. This, of course, led ultimately to the collapse of the bank, which would have been utterly disastrous had it not been for the intervention of the Bank of England. The point here is that something as simple as a brand promise on trust, if it is betrayed in any way, can lead to a complete collapse of the brand.

Another example was the Arthur Andersen accountancy firm—probably, at the time, the largest accountancy firm in the world—which became caught up in the great financial scandals of corporate America and ultimately completely and utterly collapsed. Arthur Andersen, a large accounting firm that audits other companies, had to be seen to be whiter than white.

DEFINING WHAT IT IS AND STICKING TO IT

As we look at the whys and wherefores and the can-dos and can-nots of developing your brand, let us turn now to your own brand. What does it stand for right now? In particular, is what it stands for consistent with the vision you have for it as you move your business forward? Have you got a brand mission statement—in other words, have you articulated in writing what the essence of your business is? When we started up the O'Briens business, our brand mission statement was to sell good-quality sandwiches and coffee from an Irish-themed environment by way of franchised retail outlets, with our franchise partners being the most successful in the industry. Many years later these same ideas and values permeate the business, as we now re-position ourselves for the years ahead. The business has changed—the environment certainly has—but offering quality and service at a good price hasn't.

Working out what your brand mission statement is isn't always an easy thing to do, and you may make many attempts at it before you get something you are happy with. But it is worth working on it, because when you do get it, it is a really valuable thing to have as it provides absolute clarity about what it is you are trying to do. That is good for you and good for stakeholders in the business, because then you are all singing from the same hymn sheet.

Of course, having a mission statement that is ignored in the business is worse than having none at all. How many times have you been in the reception area of a business and seen a high-falutin', grand-looking mission statement framed on the wall, when it is more than obvious from your dealings with the business that nobody lives by it.

BEING THE BRAND GUARDIAN

As the business founder or driver, you have a clear sense of where you want to take the business. No one else in the organisation will feel quite the same way as you do. Having articulated your vision through your brand mission statement, and assuming it encompasses your passion and your beliefs, then you become almost like a policeman for the brand. If you really believe that your mission statement is the way forward for you, then you need to be relentless about making sure it is followed by the people who work with you; you need to be bloody-minded about sticking to it (assuming of course that you are not flogging a dead horse), and that means you need to be uncompromising about changing it.

For example, as the business develops, people both within and outside the company will suggest ways for you to take the business forward. In our business, the perennial suggestion is, 'In our town/city/country the people like to eat chips/fries with their sandwiches. If only we could sell chips/fries we would be unbelievably successful.' Well, as our brand guardian, I have a problem with that. I think our business should be about freshly prepared food that's *good* for you. Deep-fried food forms no part of that experience, and even though I want to please the people I work with, we'll be selling chips in O'Briens *over my dead body*!

WRITING DOWN HOW IT IS TO BE REPRODUCED AND IN WHAT CONTEXT

While this won't be relevant for every business, if you are going to reproduce the visual essence of your brand, you need to specify exactly how you want it reproduced so others can copy that. For example, if you are printing paper bags to put your goods in, you need to articulate exactly the colour in which you want your logo reproduced, in what position, in what size and against what background. The same applies to your stationery: you need to think about your letterheads: in what way your logo will be reproduced; in what size; in what colour; in what position on the paper and with what background.

Knowing what you want your brand to achieve is the first step in building it into a *great* brand.

Brody's 3 ideas on branding

- Under-promise and over-deliver
- Make sure your actions are consistent with your brand values
- Write down and articulate what your brand is about

Chapter 13

Where are you with IT?

Seven or eight years ago in our O'Briens business we decided to upgrade our cash register system. Our old system had been around a long time and consisted of a basic cash register which printed a till receipt. At the end of every day we were able to do a reading off the till which gave us our notional sales figure, from which we were able to work out our cash. It was a low-cost but reliable system that worked. We decided as a progressive company that we should move with the times, in particular that we should move in tune with what other retailers were doing. All other serious retailers were moving to what is known as an Electronic Point of Sale (EPOS) system, and we didn't want to get left behind.

The theoretical benefits of an EPOS system were clear: we could do away with our old manual system; we could get direct sales reports into our support office at any time of the day from any store; and it would have the added benefit of being able to analyse the cost of inputs so that we could keep an eye on our margins.

So we commissioned a system, both hardware and software, and proceeded to install it in our stores.

To say it was problematic was an understatement. Some aspects of it turned out to be either very laborious or time-consuming. We had huge problems getting the connectivity right from our individual stores into our support office. It was just too much hassle to try and work out the cost-of-sale element from the cash register. In short, we hadn't given an adequate brief to our installers, and the system was far too complicated. What should have taken two years to put in turned into four, with a lot of unhappy staff and disgruntled franchisees along the way. It took us that long to get the basics right so that we could start using it as a tool to develop the business. It didn't have to be like that.

The story of the installation of our IT system is a good example of what can go wrong with IT even in a relatively small business. Keeping that in mind, this chapter will try to guide you towards the things you should look at and should be watching for as you develop the business—when it probably isn't at the heart of what you are doing. You see, as businesses become technically more complex, there is a much greater capacity for a major disaster.

So what is IT exactly? Well, IT is everything to do with technology in your company—from computer hardware and software to the phone system. In a retail business like ours, it also encompasses an electronic point of sale system (EPOS). IT is to do with your office equipment like franking machines and copiers but also your printers, your Personal Digital Assistant (PDA) like a BlackBerry®, and, of course, mobile phones. Trying to keep an overview of all these different items and their effectiveness (and usefulness), the cost and the technology as it becomes available is very time-consuming but necessary. So let us look at some of the aspects of IT that can affect your business and that you should keep a watching brief on. Let us look at what you are doing now, what equipment you are using, what software you are using, and have a look at the possibility of changing it or operating it in the period ahead.

RISK

Let us first look at some of the risk areas in the IT area and the general things you should be watching out for so that you don't get in trouble.

Disaster recovery

Imagine if you had a serious fire in your place of work, or your computers got stolen or indeed the building was flooded. What implications would this have for the operation of your business? For a lot of businesses this would be a huge internal problem and, indeed, for a lot of small businesses that has just been the case. A disaster recovery plan is one in which you write down what you would do in the event of a major disaster happening, but, more importantly, the plan will also throw up preventative measures you can take to make sure you are not completely screwed.

So, for example, the backing up of the hard drive on your computer at the end of every day, or at least at the end of every week, and keeping that back-up copy off the premises means that in the unlikely event of something happening to your computers, you won't be completely hung out to dry, as you would be if you had no back-up and no record of what's been happening.

Legal risks

Becoming an employer gets more and more onerous, and there are a number of legal risk areas associated with IT that you need to be aware of. You need to make the appropriate adjustments to your business to make sure you are not caught on the hop. Some of these are:

- Appropriate internet usage—making sure that people are not using your business internet to access inappropriate material, for example, pornography, is a fairly basic issue nowadays which is usually covered by an appropriate clause in your staff manuals.

- E-mail etiquette—advising your staff what is appropriate and what is not appropriate in terms of their e-mail usage is also important. For example, circulating defamatory or derogatory comments about another member of staff is unacceptable, never mind the danger of circulating or distributing commercially sensitive information outside the business.
- Data protection—the keeping of information and records like a sales database is now covered by a Data Protection Act and you need to ensure that you are complying with the terms of the Act regarding the information you are storing on individuals.
- Hacking and viruses—any computer user nowadays is aware of the dangers of hacking or viruses affecting your computer or indeed your network of computers. Keeping the latest anti-viral software up to date is essential, and limiting the ability of an outsider to access your computer system by putting a firewall in place is now a fairly basic requirement.

YOUR WEBSITE

I am an absolute believer that websites are not a necessity for every business, but if you are one of the growing number for whom it is, it says everything about you and your business. In that sense you have to get it as right as you can. You should also consider building it in such a way that you can maintain and update it yourself rather than having to farm it out to a more expensive website development company. An absolute essential requirement for websites is that your contact details are easily available. I cannot tell you the number of websites that I look at where I am looking for a postal address or number but can't actually find them anywhere. The only way you can contact the company is by sending e-mail, and often that is not what I am looking to do at all.

Separating myth from reality

There is a myth about that it's impossible to function in modern business without having your own website. That may be true for some businesses, but for many it's not true at all. Lots of businesses cope effectively with no website or at best a very limited, low-maintenance one.

Having an appropriate web presence for your business (if you need one at all) is the trick.

Clearly if you're actually selling a product over the web, you need a much more sophisticated site than, say, a business which is using the web as an information resource for potential customers (for example, a restaurant showing sample menus as well as directions to the building).

A few ideas that have struck me about websites are as follows:

Their importance is often overstated

A lot of business owners expect too much from a web presence. Usually it's part of a marketing mix, but not the whole story. For instance, to sell a franchise in O'Briens we think it's important to have a web presence (people who want to find out about us get instant information), but it sits alongside our brochures, our presence at trade shows, information in our stores, talking to existing franchisees, word of mouth, PR and press adverts as only one of many ways in which we attract prospective franchisees. To rely on it solely would be a big mistake.

Search engine optimisation

This is where you pay to make sure your name appears high on search engines like Google and Yahoo. The idea is that if a person enters in a search engine words like 'sandwich', 'café', 'franchise', then our name will pop up promptly.

Make it easy to keep it up to date

There is nothing worse to my mind than an out-of-date website. It just looks unprofessional, and often I think because the website was designed to be essentially high maintenance. As your website is being thought through, keep in mind how much effort will be required to keep it up to date versus the potential rewards from it. For this reason I was never interested in doing a blog—a kind of internet diary—because I knew that it wasn't important enough to me to update it every day.

Use a third party to build it

Theoretically you could build your own website, but if that's not your business, you're better off leaving it to the professionals. Picking a company is one thing; making sure they're suitable for you to have a long-term relationship with is another matter (the website will need to be maintained). It's worth spending time trying to pick the best, because it's a pain in the ass to try and change suppliers in this area unless you're going for a totally new site.

Give a very clear brief

Many people who are unhappy with the way their website turns out are guilty of not providing a clear brief to the supplier. Writing out on an A4 page what you want the site to do is a great discipline (only one page!).

You should consult friends or business colleagues about it too, and take their input on board. If it's not your main business, it's very hard to keep up with the latest developments in the area.

After you have chosen your supplier, you need to sit down with them and go through the brief thoroughly, maybe showing examples of websites that you admire, and agree timelines that work for you both.

Provide the materials needed in a timely fashion

As part of your in-depth brief to your supplier, you should agree with them as to what material you will be supplying. You will certainly be providing photos, sales literature and text for the site. Perhaps photographs will have to be commissioned and you have to find time to compose suitable wording. Either way, be realistic about when you are going to be able to do it, and allocate sufficient time in your diary to make it happen.

Measure its usage

As part of your deal with your supplier, you should get him to install some counting software on your site that measures the traffic to individual pages. You can then see what pages are working well or not, as the case may be.

Figure out how to publicise it

Having a great website isn't much use if people don't know it's there or don't feel a need to use it. Figuring out how you can publicise it in your particular business may be a process of trial and error.

We found that, because we produce so much printed material like cups and bags, it cost us nothing to display our website address prominently to our customers.

Let us conduct a quick IT audit for your business, both hardware and software, just with a view to seeing if you are covering the obvious.

CONDUCTING A QUICK IT AUDIT

Conducting an in-depth audit of each of your IT functions is outside the scope of a book like this. However, the headings below are designed to jog your memory and stimulate your thinking.

Burglar alarms

Is there one? Is it monitored by a monitoring service so you don't have to get up in the middle of the night? Who has the code; is it time to change it? Is the system working properly?

Computer desktops and laptops

Is the equipment you are using appropriate for your particular usage? Are the computers old in the sense of having become very slow? Do the computers need to be upgraded or is it just a question of getting extra memory for them? Would having wireless access to them be a useful feature?

Printers

Printers have now become very cheap to buy. The hidden cost, however, is in the cost of consumables (cartridges). What are you paying for consumables for your printer? Is it necessary to have a separate printer and copier? How many printers or copiers do you have located in your business? Would it make more sense to centralise them to one location that everyone has access to?

Copiers

Do you have a requirement for copying in black and white or is there a colour requirement as well? If you do have a colour requirement, which for many businesses is quite small, is one colour copier enough in the business backed up by a number of black and white ones? As with printers, above, is it necessary to have separate printers and copiers?

Postal franking

Has your business grown enough now to justify a postal franking machine? If you are already using one, do you need a bigger one? Is your logo printed on your signed pieces of mail?

PABX phone system

Do you have one already? Should you consider getting one? Does the one you have need to be upgraded? What sort of features do you need on a phone system nowadays? Apart from voice messaging and auto callbacks, what else would you consider necessary? Has your system got a music feature built into it where you can play something appropriate to your business or indeed a sales message?

Mobile phones

Are the phones you are using appropriate to your usage? For example, do you need all the features of a modern phone, like cameras and video? Are you on the best tariff for your business? Have you barred inappropriate phone usage like the ability to make international calls or access to premium rate sites? If your company uses PDAs e.g. BlackBerry®, is it necessary to have a separate mobile phone as well, or could employees use just one? How many employees actually need a mobile phone for their business, because not everybody does?

Microsoft Outlook

Many of us are now using Outlook as our default e-mail programme. Even if you are not, there are a few useful guides you can think about for your e-mail usage. For example, you should encourage your staff to use the phone more often. I see so many e-mails coming across my desk which have obviously taken quite a bit of time to write where it would have actually been quicker, and you would have received a more immediate response, if you had just picked up the phone and asked the question or said what the issue was.

If there is a dispute, it is a much better idea to pick up the phone and talk to somebody rather than sending an e-mail. E-mails cannot pick up tone or inflections, and, in that sense, when you 'say' something by e-mail in the printed word, it can be totally misinterpreted. If you have something contentious that you can only say by e-mail, it is a good idea to wait for a day to see how you feel about it and reflect upon it. E-mails are often dashed off without any thought being given to them, and when something is recorded in the printed word, it can often have a long-lasting and damaging effect. A piece of advice I picked up some years ago about e-mail was that if you wouldn't be happy to have an e-mail read out in a court of law, then you shouldn't put it in writing.

Explorer

Explorer and similar programmes are used by most of us now to access the internet. The internet itself has become an indispensable resource for getting information quickly. For example, we no longer keep a list of our shop contact details as a hard copy in the office anywhere; it is kept on our website and all of us have access to the latest version. What are you using the internet for in work?

There is no doubt that many people use it inappropriately in work, whether it is looking at sites they shouldn't be looking at or indeed using it for personal activities during working time. If you operate your system on a network, it is quite possible now to keep a log of individuals' internet usage. This should be checked periodically. People can be given appropriate warnings if necessary, just to make sure it doesn't get out of hand.

Networking

If you have more than one or two computers in your office, you should probably be networked if you are not already. Networking should save time, but it also brings its own set of issues to an area where you didn't have issues before. For example, if one computer, like the server, is down, then it means all the computers are down where they weren't heretofore. You will probably also hold your databases and information centrally, which means they may not be easily accessed by somebody who is outside the office, whereas previously they may have had all that information on their laptop, which they could carry with them. Security of the information in your system becomes an issue when your system is networked. Are you taking the steps necessary to ensure that appropriate people have access to the appropriate parts of your system? Are you changing the access passwords regularly?

Accounts package

If you are not already using an accounts package, is it time for you to consider getting one? If you are already using one, is the package you are using appropriate for your business as you plan for the years ahead? Are you qualified to make that kind of decision yourself or do you need some outside help, perhaps from your accountants or auditors, as to what sort of package you actually need? It is well worth sitting down and writing out a brief of what you want or expect from your software package before you approach different sellers. This will ensure you get exactly what you want as opposed to being sold something that may not be suitable for your needs.

Database

Most of us now run databases for lots of different areas of our business. So, for example, information on your staff would be in one particular database, information on customers on another, information on prospective customers on yet another database. Are you using a specific database package to run these or are you using a programme like Microsoft Excel? If so, is that appropriate for your needs? Do you need further training in the use of, for example, Microsoft Excel, or more information on the database packages that are available? Modern database packages, particularly on the sales side, now come under the Customer Relationship Management (CRM) heading. Should you be using a CRM package for your sales database?

PDA

Are you using PDAs in your business? Should you be using them and, if you should, who should have them? Can your PDA be combined with a phone? How are you going to link your PDAs into the networking system in the office?

Setting up an IT department

Is it appropriate for you now to be setting up an IT department and employing an IT manager? Should you bring the management and maintenance of your website in-house or is it more appropriate to keep it with an outside supplier? What would you actually like an IT department to do in your business in an ideal world?

Brody's 3 ideas on IT

- Conduct an IT audit on your business
- Put a disaster recovery plan in place
- Ban the use of e-mails in a dispute

Chapter 14
How to Deal with Suppliers

Of all the areas we study in business, the least worked on or understood is that between your business and your suppliers. I suppose it's because on the surface it's so easy. In comparison to securing sales for your products or building a good team around you, finding a company willing to supply you is usually easy. But a good supplier, one who understands what you are trying to do and supports you in that, can be as important to your business as anything else.

I don't know how you find dealing with them, but I have made some really basic mistakes in my dealings where I have kicked myself later as a result. Here follow some ideas and tips for suppliers in general—and for some in particular—of various goods and services to your business, to help you get the best out of the relationship. These are based on bitter and often expensive experience that we have gone through. It is not an exhaustive list, but there should be some nuggets in here to help you save money.

GENERAL HINTS WHEN SPENDING YOUR COMPANY'S MONEY

Shopping around

Even though common sense would dictate that you shop around, surprisingly few of us bother to do so. We get into a relationship with a supplier initially and we are happy to accept what he says is his price as being effectively non-negotiable.

It always pays to shop around and particularly to let your existing supplier know that they don't have an exclusive supply arrangement with you. Even if you think it is a good idea to stay with your existing supplier (for a variety of reasons), it does no harm at all to keep him or her on their toes by having a more competitive quote from one of their competing suppliers.

Include suppliers in your planning

Including your suppliers in your planning is one of those common-sense things that you find out only after going through a negative experience. In the early days of O'Briens, I remember running a promotion on what were then new-fangled wraps or Wrappos™ as we call them. Wrappos are tortilla pancakes that have become popular as a low-fat, low-calorie alternative to bread. The promotion involved a very successful two-for-one offer where, if you bought one, you got a second one free. It worked really well for us, and when we ran the promotion we sold tons of them. The only problem was that we had forgotten to let our supplier know that we expected to use substantially more than we normally did, and the supplier very quickly ran out of the product. We found ourselves in a situation where we had created demand for a product that we couldn't satisfy, and we ended up creating lots of problems for ourselves as well as creating bad-will (the opposite of good!) with our customers; if we had taken the trouble to include our suppliers in our planning process, that wouldn't have happened.

Leaving aside a basic requirement like making sure your supplier has sufficient stock to satisfy your promotion, including your suppliers in your planning will make them feel more like part of the family, and if their relationship with you is closer than it is with other customers, it follows that they are likely to look after you better.

We made it a cornerstone of our business some years ago to invite our suppliers to our annual conference, effectively to run a sub-conference for them where we brought them up to speed on what we were doing and what our plans were. As a result of this, we forged some very close and lasting relationships that served us well during some difficult times.

Understand the difference between regular and irregular suppliers

Regular suppliers are ones that you deal with continuously, like raw material suppliers, accountants, the phone company etc. Irregular ones are those you deal with only once or rarely. Examples of these might be builders or carpet suppliers or architects. It follows that the relationship you have with each will be different. Regular suppliers are those you will want to train and develop and have a long-term relationship with. Irregular ones are different and you should rely more on references and testimonials when choosing these. These are also easier to change.

Give them your budget and let them know it's real

How often does it happen, particularly with suppliers like architects, that you give them a budget to do up a shop, for example, only to find that they treated the budget you gave them with disdain and came in with a design that costs more to build than your budget allows? If you are not mindful of this, it can get you into hot water immediately. This is particularly relevant to a newer business where cash is critical and budgeting is likely to be wrong anyway—the added burden of an unrealistic design can just tip you that bit further over the edge than you need to be.

It stands to reason that you need to make your supplier understand that if you give them a budget, it is a real budget; it is not a made-up number, and this is the number they need to work to.

Take up references

It's always worth taking up references, but especially when you are spending large sums of money. If, for example, you are moving to a larger premises, with all the expense involved, it's well worth your while to ask for and take up references, particularly from suppliers like builders, shop-fitters etc. A good builder should also have no problem letting you actually see the last few jobs he has completed, so you can judge the standards of finishes etc.

Ask for prices upfront—especially from accountants and lawyers

As your business grows you are likely to be using professional services like accountants and lawyers more regularly than you did at the start-up stage. As your business grows you tend to use the bigger firms who tend to give a more professional and more in-depth service, and you may find, as we did, that the bills you start getting in are truly outrageous. Your perception of what seems to be a relatively small job, by the time the accountants or lawyers have got stuck into it, has mushroomed into something that is really quite far beyond what you had expected, and this can be particularly costly if the accountants or lawyers have done work on a speculative project that hasn't ended up going ahead.

There is a story doing the rounds in Dublin about a successful businessman who, when he goes in for a meeting with his lawyers, places a large stopwatch on the table. He opens the meeting by asking how everybody's family is, how business is going, a general discussion about the weather, and he then asks if anybody would like to go to the toilet.

Once he has established that all the small talk is over and nobody needs to go to the toilet, he hits the start button on his stopwatch. About half an hour into the meeting one of the lawyers indicated that he would like to use the bathroom, and our businessman stamps his hand on the stopwatch. He then asks if anyone else in the meeting would like to go to the toilet, as now is the time to go. At the end of the meeting our business-man gets the lawyers to sign a piece of paper saying exactly how many minutes have been used. The story, I'm sure, has been exaggerated to make a point, but it is a good point. If you make your accountants and lawyers aware that you are watching the clock, and if you go to the trouble of getting them to give you a price (even a general price if they can't be absolutely specific, but before they start the work), it tends to keep some sense on the price arrived at, and you're not going to be in for a nasty surprise.

It's incredibly difficult to work out if you are being charged the correct amount by your lawyers or accountants because so much of the work they do is not directly related to the meeting you may have attended but is 'behind the scenes work' that you are probably not really conscious of.

Negotiate the important points before you part with your money

It is often the case when you do a deal with a supplier that, with the euphoria of agreeing the major points and agreeing to do a deal, the smaller points get overlooked or left for later to tidy up. Inevitably, leaving things to be sorted out later will lead to problems—memories become rusty or the relationship develops. People 'remember' what was informally agreed to suit their own particular agenda. I think it is well worthwhile signing a Memorandum of Understanding with a supplier which attempts to cover exactly the fine print of what your business arrangement means. Having also agreed the important issue of a price, you should now agree under what circumstances the price can change, the delivery methods, the delivery times, the payment terms, and other such items which may appear trivial at the time.

Give a proper briefing for the job to be done

How often do we instruct a supplier to go ahead with a particular job when we haven't really thought through what we want them to do, or the supplier doesn't understand fully what we want them to do?

For example, if you are briefing a website designer on how to build a new website for you, you need to be quite specific inasmuch as you can be about what you want that site to achieve, and how you want it to be achieved. Otherwise the website designer may not completely understand what is in your head and could come up with his own interpretation of what he thinks you said, which inevitably will lead to problems.

Say thank you

Having a good relationship with your supplier, which can be all-important when the chips are down or a problem occurs, is dependent at the end of the day on realising that your suppliers are human just like yourself. Suppliers aren't any different to you in that they appreciate a sincere thank you and recognition for a job well done. You can't say thank you often enough, whether it is to customers for their business or suppliers for their service.

INSURANCE

Know what is in your policies

Not long after O'Briens started business we had a solicitor's letter from a reputable law firm in town, written on behalf of one of their clients. The lady had apparently gone into an O'Briens store and purchased a piece of carrot cake. She had consumed half of it before she realised there was blue mould on the back of it. The letter claimed that the client had become very ill after eating it and was looking for a substantial sum in damages.

Now I was aware that blue mould, albeit unsightly and not fit to be served up, is unlikely to make you ill when consumed in small quantities. So I was outraged at the demand for substantial compensation. This happened at the height of our 'compo culture' in Ireland when stories were appearing in the papers daily about companies being ripped off by fraudulent claims—with a consequent hike in insurance premiums.

I decided to take a stand on the basis that no honest judge would compensate such an audacious claim. The day arrived when we went to court, and our customer came up in front of the judge. By the time her testimony had finished, she had not only become ill from consuming the dodgy carrot cake but had also become agoraphobic and could not leave the house. Her daughter had had a miscarriage because of the stress caused and, again because of the stress, her husband had had to give up his job. What had been a fairly trivial incident had mushroomed into something quite extraordinary. I sat at the back of the court quite confident that the judge would throw out this ridiculous story. But the judge didn't; the judge awarded the lady the substantial compensation she was looking for, which I had to pay. Later that night when I was recounting that miserable day to a friend, he said to me, 'Surely you were insured for that?' Sure enough, when I went to check, I was insured for it but because I hadn't reported it to the insurance company, and because I had decided to go to court and fight the case myself, they didn't want anything to do with it and I was left to pay the sum myself. It was doubly painful—handing the money over for a ridiculous claim for which I was actually insured. I needn't have taken on the financial grief—not only the compensation, but also the cost of briefing a lawyer and barrister—particularly at a time when I had no money.

The second moral to take from the story is to avoid going to court at all costs. What seems at the time to be a morally sound position can often cost substantially more than the original grievance is worth. But you also have no certainty of the outcome, and the law can sometimes make a complete mockery of natural justice.

Understand your risks and take steps to reduce them

In the early days of O'Briens we had a reasonably frequent occurrence of staff members cutting their fingers on our meat slicer. Now at the time we were using big meat slicers with a circular blade that went around very quickly. If the staff were handling, for example, a cut of cold meat from the fridge, and they got distracted at all, they could actually run their finger through the slicer along with the cut of meat. It became a problem that was occurring too frequently, and often gave rise to an insurance claim.

We thought about what we could do about this predicament, and decided that we would ask our suppliers to pre-slice the meat before it was delivered into the shop and we could therefore phase out the meat slicers. This worked well and so we solved the problem and it hasn't occurred again since. It also had the added benefit of reducing our labour costs, as this time-consuming job of slicing the meat was passed back to our suppliers instead.

Take the time to train your staff

You can save yourself a lot of problems by training your staff well—in our case we need to cover basic food hygiene, and more generally businesses should cover health and safety, equipment operation etc. Apart from the fact that you have a duty of care to your staff, it will also impress your insurance company and may ensure they give you a lower premium than they otherwise might.

LEGAL MATTERS

Learn how to say sorry

How often does a relatively minor dispute escalate into something much more serious, simply because the situation wasn't handled very well? We have had numerous situations over the years where a customer became upset about the way their complaint was dealt with in the store and then decided to take legal action as a result.

Teaching your staff how to say sorry can alleviate much distress. A customer who has a genuine complaint, and who then makes a complaint to a member of staff, rightfully expects the issue to be handled correctly and sensitively. If the complaint is handled well and properly, 99 per cent of the time it means the customer will leave the premises feeling better about the business than they had in the first place. This may seem ironic, but it shows the customer that the store management and the store staff are reasonable people, and they tend to not want to pursue them legally through the courts.

Go to court at your peril

I have only been to court three times with the business for commercial disputes, one of which was the mouldy carrot cake referred to earlier. We lost every case, and it cost us money. My limited experience of courts says go to court at your absolute peril. Find another way to settle a dispute but don't go to court, particularly in cases involving consumers. The courts, it would appear, tend to err on the side of the individual and against the big fat cat company who is making money off the back of the exploited customer.

Consider using different lawyers for different purposes

Here in Ireland I use three different lawyers depending on what job we want done. For everything to do with our important franchising work, which is technically quite difficult and absolutely vital to the long-term prosperity of the business, we use one of the big law firms, who charge top dollar for it. We feel it is worth paying top dollar for something that could potentially bring the whole company down if it is not dealt with properly. We use another firm for conveyancing and low-level legal disputes, and that seems to work quite well. Finally, I use a family lawyer for family work—moving house, making a will etc.

GENERAL SUPPLIERS

Be realistic but optimistic when producing projected business levels

When dealing with a new supplier for the first time, you are often tempted to overstate what level of business a supplier will do with you, on the basis that with increased volumes he will give you a better price. That is partly true, but if you grossly overstate the level of business that the supplier can do, it is not fair to him and ultimately it won't be fair to you. This is because if the supplier overbuys in the expectation of doing a huge level of business with you, and then ends up not doing it, he will lose money, which he will have to pass on to you in higher prices.

It pays to be realistic but optimistic, so err on the positive side of your projections, but not to the point where they become ridiculous.

Educate suppliers about your business

Educating your supplier about how your business works is just one of those common-sense things we should do but tend not to. For example, explaining to your supplier that you don't want any deliveries made between the hours of 12:00 and 14:00 when you are in the lunchtime food business seems obvious, but how often do we neglect to tell suppliers that? Talking to your supplier about your business, about the seasonal highs and lows, about what way you would like to be invoiced and how frequently, what your policy is on deliveries, checking in deliveries and returns, how you will pay them—these all make for a better business relationship. They are things that should be established at the outset of a new relationship with a supplier.

Give yourself a target to reduce your numbers

One of the ways you can become more efficient in your business is by reducing the number of suppliers delivering into you. So, for example, in our fresh food business, we had a situation when we started off having quite a large number of suppliers delivering quite small amounts of product. For example, we had a meat supplier, a cheese supplier, a dairy supplier and a dry goods supplier all delivering in separately, as well as a cake supplier and a biscuit supplier. At one of our conferences we got our suppliers together and said to them, 'Look, why not co-operate among yourselves? Instead of each of you delivering to 60 outlets once a week, why not come to some arrangement between yourselves where you make one delivery into one supplier, who is going to do all the deliveries to all the shops?' This made a lot of sense to some of the suppliers, and they were able to pass on a portion of their savings to us after they had paid the main supplier, who was going to be doing the distribution at a cost for the extra trouble he was taking.

The main supplier was happier too, as he had the truck delivering anyway, and now he could make extra sales and margins from the same trip.

It made a lot of sense for us as well, as we reduced the number of deliveries coming into the store and we reduced the time it took to check the stuff in. We also reduced the number of invoices we were receiving and the number of payments we had to make. Everyone became a winner.

As a result of that we introduced a rule internally that we will never increase the number of food suppliers into the business. Our target is to slowly reduce the number one by one, so we end up with perhaps one fresh goods supplier who does everything fresh, one dry goods supplier who does everything non-perishable, and one packaging supplier who does every-thing else—three suppliers instead of the 12 we have right now. We still have a way to go and we may never get there, but this policy does help guide our purchasing arrangements.

BUILDERS

A bottle of whiskey
It pays to have a relationship with your builders and look after them as a job is being done. While most competent builders

won't need day-to-day supervision in a job, it does no harm for you to drop in from time to time to measure progress on the job and to say thank you to the builder as he is doing a good job (assuming of course he is). As a job nears its conclusion, problems often arise where extras need to be done which you hadn't anticipated paying for, or it could be that the job is taking longer than the builder anticipated and he is losing money over it. At this critical time, it makes sense to try and keep the relationship right. As the builder nears completion, even if there are bits outstanding, recognise that fact by perhaps giving a bottle of whiskey or some gesture to say thank you for a job well done.

The reason for doing this is that if you end up on good terms with your builder, he is much more likely to come back and sort problems later. If your relationship has fallen apart, however, and there is an atmosphere of mutual hostility, wild horses probably won't drag him back to finish the job.

Stage your payments

Clearly, it makes sense to give your builder a financial incentive to finish your job properly, and so it makes sense to stage your payments. We have found it works quite well for us to pay our builder 50 per cent on signing a contract to do a job, 40 per cent on practical completion and ten per cent when the snag list is completed. The ten per cent should effectively be the builder's profit on the job, so you are not affecting his cash flow. And he has a substantial incentive to go back and finish the job properly.

ACCOUNTANTS

Agree fees in advance for statutory work

Standard jobs that you need an accountant to do, like filing your annual returns or completing your annual audit, are jobs that your accountant or auditor can do with a fair degree of accuracy. For that reason he shouldn't have any issue with giving you a price in advance to get that job done, and it is worth your while agreeing that with him before an appointment is made.

It follows that for other work where it is more difficult to give an estimate—maybe the length of the work is a movable feast or the level of work isn't known entirely—you should agree with your accountant that new work can only proceed when you have agreed the cost in advance.

Brody's 3 ideas on suppliers

- Train suppliers on how you like to do business
- Go to court at your peril
- Say thank you

Chapter 15

Corporate Social Responsibility—Making Money by Doing the Right Thing

There is something going on in our business world.

You remember when sports goods giant Nike faced an extensive consumer boycott after the *New York Times* reported on abusive labour practices that Nike was involved with in Asia. As a result of that, Nike had to tidy up their act and change those practices.

Remember also global oil giant Shell's decision to sink the Brent Spar oil rig in the North Sea, which sparked Greenpeace protests and headlines around the world. Those of us in Ireland will also be familiar with Shell's headlines in the newspapers and on the television around trying to bring a gas pipeline ashore in Co. Mayo, where locals objected strenuously to the proposed development.

Have you noticed the little sign in the bathrooms in hotels you stay in? The signs have messages on them asking you to save detergent and electricity by reusing your towel instead of getting a fresh one every day. Some of us look at those signs with a degree of cynicism.

What about global food companies like Nestlé and Kraft with their Fairtrade coffee? For years these companies were among the largest coffee purchasers in the world on the most exploit-ative terms. Why is it they are suddenly getting all responsible?

What about our government ministers buying carbon offsets for their travel abroad and particularly our 'green' ministers driving around now in a Toyota Prius to show their green credentials?

I attended Ireland's first carbon-neutral conference this year which was organised by global accounting firm Ernst & Young to demonstrate their concern for the environment.

Corporate Social Responsibility (CSR) is happening in a big way now and savvy companies are waking up to that fact.

WHAT IS CSR?

CSR has been defined as a business approach that creates long-term shareholder value by embracing opportunities and managing risks associated with environmental, economic and social development. To put it another way, companies who continue to ignore it are on a road to declining profits and shareholder value.

Customers want a deeper relationship with businesses. Consumers are increasingly interested in taking action on social issues, whether that is reducing air miles by buying their food at the local farmers' market, sending goats to Africa instead of presents for themselves, buying from a local business instead of a multinational, or eating organically. Our customers are changing—changing the way they behave and, most importantly, the way they shop.

People want to work for companies that they feel good about. In today's terms that not only means companies that do great products but also companies that have a reputation for taking their responsibilities as good corporate citizens seriously. Our employees want to feel good about themselves and the part they play in their companies over and above the actual technical job. This is the age of meaning and increasingly those who want to work with us are the sort of people who seek meaning from their employment also.

Companies that are cottoning on to this are doing better. Good CSR practices add to the bottom line.

WHY AREN'T MORE COMPANIES DOING IT?

So, if we are in charge of running a company or working in a company, we know we should be doing something about it. We know intellectually it makes sense; we know our competitors are looking at it or are already doing it; we know it is becoming more important as a tool to retain the best people; and we know customers think it is important enough to affect their purchasing decisions. Yet, as we also know, lots of us are not doing it. Why is that? What is holding us back?

Because we are afraid of the unknown. A study for the Prince of Wales Trust in the UK listed the top eight reasons companies don't get involved in CSR and they were:

- It costs money and therefore will reduce profitability especially in the short term
- A business's main responsibility is to its shareholders
- It is not the job of businesses to support social causes; that is the job of government
- It will be seen as a superficial marketing tool by customers
- It will take our eye off the ball
- We don't know what to do
- It won't make any difference
- Often the performance of companies in the CSR space does not match the public's expectations

These fears are completely natural, but look at what the research shows us are the benefits:

- Extra sales
- Improved staff retention
- Increase in customer loyalty
- Greater profits
- Increased shareholder value

MY FIRST TASTE OF CSR

Many of you in Ireland will remember the summer of 2003. It was the summer of the Special Olympics. Up and down the country people from all walks of life got involved in trying to make the Games as successful as they could be. Thousands of people and hundreds of companies got involved. For many of those people and many of those companies, they would say it was one of the best things they had ever done. It was a fantastic national effort and I remember so well standing in Croke Park in Dublin the night of the Opening Ceremony, my heart bursting with pride because I had been part of making it happen.

A couple of years before that—I think around 2001—I had seen a documentary on TV about the Special Olympic Games which had been held in North Carolina in 1999. The documentary was being shown because it had just been announced that Ireland was to host the Games in 2003. I remember watching that documentary; I have a bit of an interest in that area because I have a couple of godchildren with learning disabilities. I remember I was watching—really with my commercial hat on—thinking, you know, this is going to be huge in Ireland; this is going to be really successful; this would be a great thing for O'Briens to be associated with. You see, I thought that getting our name up in lights with other big sponsors would really take us from being a small local brand into a real national brand. At the time we were operating in seven countries and I was conscious that the Special Olympics were involved in all these countries as well, and therefore it was an appropriate project to support because all our people, in whatever country we were operating, could get involved in it. Anyway, I looked at this documentary, a bit like a lot of people here, and I thought I really must do something about it. And for some strange reason, the very next day I did. I picked up the phone and I rang Denis O'Brien, who was the chairman of the Organising Committee and who had been featured in the programme the previous night, and I said to him that we wanted to get involved as a sponsor. And indeed we did. Not long afterwards, we signed up for a sponsorship of €1.25 million at a time when we couldn't have written a cheque for €10,000. In fact we became the first sponsor to officially commit to the project.

That was me crossing the threshold—by our actions we define ourselves. I had been talking about doing this kind of thing for ages, but for all the reasons we have looked at above, I had done nothing about it. But for some reason, on this occasion, through a mad impulse, I did.

Well, the Special Olympics did for us exactly what it said on the tin—it delivered what we expected in the sense that we took O'Briens from being a regional brand in Dublin and Cork to being a proper national brand. We discovered that a lot of our customers had a great deal of empathy for people with mental disability and mental handicap, because members of their own families or friends' families had a mental disability or handicap. And these customers—at least a large number of them—voted with their feet by coming in and buying more from us, so our sales went up. Our bottom line went up as well—we made more money that year than we had in previous years.

It had, however, benefits over and above branding that we didn't understand at the time. It brought all our stakeholders together—our customers, as I said, voted with their feet and came and shopped with us in ever greater numbers; a lot of our staff, who might otherwise have left the company and moved on as young people do nowadays, stayed because they felt better about the company they were working for; they took great pride in the work we were doing over and above making money, and they got involved enthusiastically in trying to make a success of it.

It cemented relationships with a lot of our suppliers as well because we got them excited and enthusiastic about it, and so they took part and gave as much of themselves and of their companies as they possibly could. It also enhanced our relationships with our franchisees because we devised ways in which they could get involved in their local community, and build their business as a result. It seems to me, when we look back on it, that we were working for something greater than ourselves. The people involved in our business felt connected, gave more of themselves to the project but also to the business, and because of that we made more money.

Our involvement with the Special Olympics came to an end in the summer of 2003. Now that I had tasted what CSR was like for me and my company and the people around me, I wanted more. It made complete commercial sense for the business and it made complete sense for me as a person. It is funny now looking back on it, but it was easily the most satisfying thing I had ever done. Yes, I had experienced huge highs over the years in the business, but with this project I had found some meaning for my life outside of the business—I had found some meaning for me as a person.

I knew from our Special Olympics experience that it wasn't enough to go at it frantically as we had with that project—it had to be better planned and it had to be sustainable. I wanted also to integrate CSR into our business strategy just as we did with our sales, our operations, our new product development, so that it would become part of what we do rather than an exceptional one-off effort.

So we researched CSR and what we felt we could be good at. We explored how other organisations do it and the lessons they had learnt. We questioned ourselves about why we were doing it and what we wanted to get out of it for the business and, as importantly, what we wanted to get out of it for ourselves.

I asked myself what am I good at—what talents do I have that could be exploited in the new project? What do I do that could be useful to someone else?

Out of this searching came some initial ideas. We didn't want to give money *per se*. We wanted to give of ourselves. Giving money doesn't turn me on—leverage does. How could I—how could we—leverage our skills and our contact base to help others? I know a bit about selling sandwiches and a bit about running a franchise and I have some experience in running a business. What I give must be me—my ideas, my values, my commitment. What our company gives must be ourselves—our values, our commitment.

For a long time I had been ashamed of and disillusioned about the efforts to end poverty in the developing world. We decided to focus our efforts on trying to do something about that and this is what we did.

CASE STUDY—CONNECT ETHIOPIA

Along with some like-minded friends who worked in other companies, we set up an organisation called Connect Ethiopia. We set it up a couple of years ago with the intention of trying to twin the business community in Ireland with the business community in Ethiopia. Here's why. Countries like Ethiopia are very poor because of the very low level of economic activity there. There may be lots of reasons for this—being in a bad neighbourhood, poor governance, corruption—but the essential fact remains the same. It seems to us that despite all the great work, the goodwill, the money and the work of non-governmental organisations (NGOs) over the years, they fail to address this fundamental issue; in effect, the work of NGOs is like sticking a plaster on the wound but not really fixing what causes the illness. You see, I have a core belief that it is not the sticking plaster of charity that works, it is the long-term stimulation of business and economic activity. Look at Ireland if you are looking for a case in point. Thirty years ago we were not a rich country. I left school in 1979. Of a class of 40 pupils, 34 emigrated. How different things are in Ireland now.

We think that if economic activity can be stimulated in a country like Ethiopia, like it was in Ireland, then that in turn will look after the other problems they experience by default, like dirty water or food security or building schools. I wanted to try and help Ethiopia by stimulating the economy, one person at a time.

So if that seems like a good idea, what can be done about it? Firstly, we thought about breaking the problem down into bite-sized pieces—the old management analogy of eating an elephant comes to mind. Ireland can't save the world, but maybe if it concentrated its resources in one country, it might make an appreciable difference. Hence the idea of Connect Ethiopia— taking the business community in Ireland, the different business sectors here, and getting them and the people involved to engage with their counterparts in Ethiopia to try to stimulate entrepreneurial activity.

We try to get different groups like accountants and bankers, coffee retailers like ourselves, textile importers, e-commerce professionals—think of all the headings in the Golden Pages— to visit Ethiopia, help upskill their profession, mentor existing Ethiopian companies, help new start-up companies, invest in/do business with and generally help them become more commercial, so that they themselves have a better chance of generating jobs and wealth.

To back that up we are arranging for industry representative bodies like the Law Society or the Bankers' Federation or Chambers of Commerce etc. to twin with their counterparts and help upskill them on an industry-wide basis.

We're really trying to engage all of the business community here, to show them, to show us, that we can make a difference— if we focus on just doing what we're good at.

So think about that:

- One rich country (Ireland) helping one poor country (Ethiopia)
- One business community in Ireland helping the business community in Ethiopia
- One industry representative body (e.g. banking) helping their counterpart body in Ethiopia
- One business (e.g. restaurant business like O'Briens) helping a restaurant business in Ethiopia
- One businessperson (like me) helping one businessperson there

And whatever they want help in:

- Knowledge transfer—letting them know how we do things in our sophisticated western economy
- Training in the latest best practice
- Mentoring individuals and businesses, as we were mentored ourselves
- Introducing them to contacts we already have who may purchase or trade with them
- Trading with them ourselves
- Even making an investment

So what we actually do is match skilled people and companies here with those who need those skills in Ethiopia. Let me tell you about one of the people who has become involved with our project. Her name is Jan O'Connell and this is her story.

My name is Jan O'Connell. I run my own photography business here in Cork. I had a tough time starting, as a lot of young businesspeople do, but it is up and running now for about 20 years and it is going well. Materially I am doing okay, but there was a bit of an emptiness inside me. I wanted to do something for other people but I didn't know what. Giving money doesn't do it for me. I heard about Connect Ethiopia from a friend and went to an information breakfast. The next thing I found myself on a plane to Ethiopia thinking what in the name of God am I doing!

Connect Ethiopia had arranged for me to run a seminar for 20 local photographers on the business of photography. This was bread-and-butter stuff for me. I wasn't so sure how to tell them what to do to be successful in commercial photography, but I had a very good idea of what they shouldn't do.

It was brilliant—the local photographers were so hungry for knowledge, and I realised I had something of real value to offer them. I spoke to them about the business of photography, about trying to specialise in particular areas, about how we charge the clients, about what sort of software we were using, about what was coming down the tracks technically, and about how to build a website. After the seminar I arranged to visit some of them at their premises. I am a real hands-on person, so when I went to visit some of these photography studios, I got stuck right into reorganising them while I was there.

I also realised that they had no representative body so the Thursday of the week I was there, I organised the inaugural meeting of the Ethiopian Professional Photographers' Association and we elected an Officer Board. This was all in four days. I felt fantastic that I had really made a difference, and I am pretty sure I will be going back.

As Jan shows us there are two types of benefit from her point of view: for her business, she is singing her involvement with Connect Ethiopia from the rooftops; she is using it to make customers and potential customers more interested in her. She reckons it is affecting, in a very positive way, her relationships with her clients and she feels she is making them more loyal; and if she makes more money as a result, well, more power to her. For Jan herself it has affected how she feels about herself and her role in this life, and she really feels she is making a difference. Let us look at a few quick examples of others.

David McKiernan runs Java Republic, which is a successful coffee roaster based in Dublin that supplies all around the country. He has made ethical sourcing the cornerstone on which he has built his business. He brings his customers out to Ethiopia for a visit, and they visit the coffee-growing regions and visit coffee farmers in person. I can tell you the loyalty he engenders from the customers he brings out is a lot more effective than any price increase he might contemplate.

Paddy Stronge was a senior banker in Bank of Ireland before he retired. He came out with us for the first time to see how he could help improve the banking and in particular the micro-finance sector. As a direct result of his visit, he persuaded the big banks here to fund a marketing project where they designed advertisements for the micro-finance banks in Ethiopia that they can use to attract depositors into their business. You see, in Ethiopia people who have money, and lots of people do, even in small amounts, are still keeping it underneath the mattress. The more money they can attract in as deposits, the more money they can lend out. Paddy also persuaded the Institute of Bankers and the Bankers' Federation here in Ireland to invite senior bankers from Ethiopia to Dublin for a visit to see how we do things here.

Wondirad Abraham is a bright businessman in Ethiopia who was looking to develop a milk business to supply milk to the city of Addis Ababa. We were able to introduce Wondirad to One51, a large Irish company with its roots in the dairy co-operative sector. One51 sent an executive to assess Wondirad's business in Ethiopia and is now considering investing in the business.

These are people and companies just like you and me. Our company and the companies involved in our project are just like your company. The difference is they decided to participate in this venture.

Whether you get involved in our Connect Ethiopia project or do your own thing by supporting a local GAA team in your area, or get your staff involved with a charity doing good work in your community or whatever, I want my message to be that you need to take the first step.

Talking about it is good; thinking about it is good; taking action is great. So today you could make a commitment to yourself, before you put this book down, that you personally and your business are going to do something about it. We would love for you to join with us in our Connect Ethiopia project; that would involve a week of your time at a cost of about €2,000 where we would bring you to that beautiful country, as part of our team, where I guarantee you would know you had made a difference.

Let's finish by looking at one more story from one of our Connectors:

I am Cathy Winston. I am an experienced executive in the business consultancy field specialising in getting companies to look at how they manage projects and communicate with each other. Recently I set up a new business with a partner, so I am flat out trying to do all the things involved in getting a new business off the ground. I had been feeling for a long time that I wanted to do something to give back. Things have been going okay for me and my boys, and I felt ready and able to give my time (at least some of it) to something other than our immediate family and business. I heard about Connect Ethiopia from friends and went on my first visit there last year. Before I went, I really wasn't sure what I could do. I was frankly a bit scared as well. The images of famine, war and drought that we were all familiar with in the 1980s had burned a really negative image in my brain. Visiting Ethiopia totally opened my eyes to what could be achieved there. I got stuck in there with 20 local tour operators who were desperate to learn. I had a fantastic time and I know I've made a difference. I realised that I am good at what I do, that I have a skill that others want to learn about, and I know it is helping these guys and girls do their business better. By enabling them to do more business, create more jobs and ultimately more wealth, I know that it will help lift all Ethiopians from poverty. It is hard to describe how I felt since then—it is as if I found a part of me that was missing—it just feels right. I am more comfortable in myself. I have got the bug now, of course. I want to do more and I will.

Getting involved in CSR is not about management—it is about leadership. Show some leadership today and get involved.

Brody's 3 ideas on CSR

- Being *good* is good business
- Figure out an angle relevant to your business
- Make CSR part of your culture

Index